CAMBRIDGE LIBRARY COLLECTION

Books of enduring scholarly value

History

The books reissued in this series include accounts of historical events and movements by eye-witnesses and contemporaries, as well as landmark studies that assembled significant source materials or developed new historiographical methods. The series includes work in social, political and military history on a wide range of periods and regions, giving modern scholars ready access to influential publications of the past.

History of the Primitive Methodist Church

Holliday Bickerstaff Kendall (1844–1919) was a Methodist minister and a social historian. Born into a family of Primitive Methodist ministers, Kendall himself served as a minister between 1864 and 1903. This volume, written during his retirement and first published in 1919, contains Kendall's history of the origins and development of the Primitive Methodist movement. The movement originated with Hugh Bourne (1772–1852) and William Clowes (1780–1851), who attempted to restore the mass evangelism they thought had been lost in the Wesleyan Church after 1810. Kendall explores the social and political context of this period, and discusses Bourne's and Clowes' influence on the origins of the movement. He then describes the growth and development of the movement in the nineteenth century, discussing the expansion of the church until 1918. This clear and concise volume is considered the definitive work on the history of the movement.

T0382369

Cambridge University Press has long been a pioneer in the reissuing of out-of-print titles from its own backlist, producing digital reprints of books that are still sought after by scholars and students but could not be reprinted economically using traditional technology. The Cambridge Library Collection extends this activity to a wider range of books which are still of importance to researchers and professionals, either for the source material they contain, or as landmarks in the history of their academic discipline.

Drawing from the world-renowned collections in the Cambridge University Library, and guided by the advice of experts in each subject area, Cambridge University Press is using state-of-the-art scanning machines in its own Printing House to capture the content of each book selected for inclusion. The files are processed to give a consistently clear, crisp image, and the books finished to the high quality standard for which the Press is recognised around the world. The latest print-on-demand technology ensures that the books will remain available indefinitely, and that orders for single or multiple copies can quickly be supplied.

The Cambridge Library Collection will bring back to life books of enduring scholarly value (including out-of-copyright works originally issued by other publishers) across a wide range of disciplines in the humanities and social sciences and in science and technology.

History of
the Primitive
Methodist Church

Holliday Bickerstaffe Kendall

CAMBRIDGE UNIVERSITY PRESS

Cambridge, New York, Melbourne, Madrid, Cape Town, Singapore,
São Paolo, Delhi, Dubai, Tokyo, Mexico City

Published in the United States of America by Cambridge University Press, New York

www.cambridge.org
Information on this title: www.cambridge.org/9781108024846

© in this compilation Cambridge University Press 2010

This edition first published 1919
This digitally printed version 2010

ISBN 978-1-108-02484-6 Paperback

HISTORY OF THE
PRIMITIVE METHODIST CHURCH.

History

of the

Primitive Methodist Church.

By
Rev. H. B. KENDALL, B.A.

(*Revised and Enlarged Edition.*)
1919.

London :
JOSEPH JOHNSON,
PRIMITIVE METHODIST PUBLISHING HOUSE,
HOLBORN HALL, CLERKENWELL ROAD, E.C.1.

THE WHITEFRIARS PRESS, LTD.,
LONDON AND TONBRIDGE.

CONTENTS

CHAPTER   PAGE

FOREWORD vii

I. ENGLAND IN 1800–32 1

II. THE WELL-HEAD OF PRIMITIVE METHODISM :

    i. The Real Beginning 11

    ii. The Methodist Camp-Meetingers . . 15

    iii. The Camp Meeting Methodists . . . 19

III. THE START OF PRIMITIVE METHODISM AND ITS COURSE TO 1819 :

    i. The Camp Meeting Methodists (*continued*) 22

    ii. William Clowes and the " Clowesites " . 23

    iii. A Pause Followed by a Swift Advance : 1811–19 30

IV. THE GEOGRAPHICAL EXTENSION OF PRIMITIVE METHODISM FROM 1819 TO 1833 . . 39

V. THE SPIRIT OF THE PIONEERS AND THEIR PROBATION OF TOIL AND SUFFERING :

    i. Our Fathers' Secret Source of Power . . 50

    ii. The Probationary Period of Toil, Privation and Persecution 57

    iii. The Crisis of 1825–8 : Its Causes and Its Lessons 66

VI. A YEASTY, TRANSITION PERIOD : 1832–60 :

    i. The " Time-spirit " of the Thirties . . 70

    ii. Extension Beyond the Seas . . . 75

    iii. A Time of Transition : Some New Departures 79

    iv. London Primitive Methodism to 1853 . 83

    v. The Jubilee Commemoration and the Sense of the Past 90

CHAPTER   PAGE

VII. THE " CONNEXION " IN MID-VICTORIAN DAYS :
1860–85 :

    i. Rough-Hewing its Future   .   .   .   93

    ii. Ministerial Training and Educational
Matters   96

    iii. Our First Missions in Africa   .   .   .   104

    iv. The Close of a Distinctly-Marked Period   .   108

VIII. MATURING CHURCH-LIFE : VARIOUS MANIFESTA-
TIONS : 1885–1897 :

    i. A Brief Conspectus of the Period   .   .   112

    ii. Some Special Developments   .   .   .   115

    iii. The Growth and Recognition of Social
Service   117

    iv. A Bold Advance into Untouched Heathendom 123

    v. The Higher Finance and Administrative
Reform   126

    vi. The Co-ordinating Conference of 1892   .   129

    vii. Development of Institutions   .   .   .   132

IX. THE CHURCH PERIOD AND THE CENTENARY YEARS :

    i. From " Connexion " to " Church "   .   .   134

    ii. The Church in Some of its External Relations   136

    iii. Some Fresh Unfoldings of Church Life   .   139

    iv. Further Development of Institutions   .   145

    v. Table of Other Notabilia of the Period
1898–1912   150

    vi. An Abiding Centenary Memorial   .   .   152

    vii. The Centenary Years   154

EPILOGUE :

    i. On-the-Eve-of-the-War Years : 1913—June
1914   160

    ii. Primitive Methodism in Time of War   .   165

APPENDICES   175

FOREWORD.

I count it an honour to write this brief foreword to this, the latest history of our Church. There must be few Primitive Methodists who are not acquainted with Mr. Kendall's smaller history published upwards of a quarter of a century ago, and with his " Principles and Polity of the Primitive Methodist Church." These little volumes, for many years, have been text-books for Local Preachers and for Ministerial Candidates. On one of my visits to the late Bishop of Durham I found these two books on the study table, and afterwards discovered that Dr. Westcott had read them with intentness and interest. The Standard History of our Church was written too by Mr. Kendall, and will immortalise his name. He was for nine years Connexional Editor, and in 1901 the President of Conference. The Book Committee felt that a smaller history was needed, bringing the story up to date. The present is practically a new volume. The historic imagination, the spiritual insight, the literary grace, which we all associate with the author, are all in evidence in these pages. The book has been written through love of the subject, with gratitude for the past, and with confidence for the future.

The mention of Mr. Kendall brings his devoted and capable wife into mind. She it is who has been at his side during long years of physical weakness, and only her wonderful care has made possible the continuance and success of his literary labours.

We greet them in this foreword, and commend the volume to all our people, and to the readers of other Churches.

JOHN G. BOWRAN,
Connexional Editor.

History of the
Primitive Methodist Church.

CHAPTER I.

England in 1800-32.

"That the power-loom, spinning-jenny, steam engine and the Primitive Methodist Revival are in time closely related is not a mere coincidence. At a grave crisis in the industrial and domestic life of the nation Primitive Methodism was instituted."

REV. T. SCRIMSHAW.

1800.—*A Convenient Starting-point.*—The year 1800 has been called "the darkest year of the century." It furnishes us with a useful and significant date-mark. At this point of time we may look round preparatory to moving on. Walter Besant, in his "London in the Eighteenth Century," makes his eighteenth century begin with 1715, and end in 1832. He is serious, and not alone, in doing this. He does not go by the almanac. Measuring a century not as a mechanical sum of years, 1801 to 1832 rather marks the close of an old order. It was a new England that was emerging after the Reform Bill and the opening years of Victoria's reign. Look where we will, it is no bright picture that meets the eye what time Primitive Methodism struggled into existence and passed through its first probationary period.

B

Philanthropy Discouraged and Exhausted.—It was on the 31st December—the last day of the eighteenth century—that the Royal Assent was given to the Act authorising the first Census of the English people. By this Act the State assumed the responsibility of knowing in " detail the vital, cultural and economic condition of the whole nation." It was high time ; for philanthropists were exhausted by past efforts and discouraged by the apparent hopelessness of the immense task before them. The masses were deplorably illiterate and the rival systems of Bell and Lancaster were unequal to the task of coping with it.   Yet the State was shy and dilatory in shouldering the responsibilities it had assumed.   Not till 1833 was a trivial school grant made of £20,000, and a timid experiment begun in public inspection.*

Hugh Bourne's Conversion.—It was in the mid-summer of 1799 Hugh Bourne joined the Methodist Church.   Books, rather than human voice or Church ordinances, had brought about the decisive change. He was first enlightened as to the nature of true religion by Wesley's sermon on the Trinity, and afterwards found peace by reading Fletcher's " Letters on the Spiritual Manifestation of the Son of God." In the year 1800, and for some time after, he tells us, he was much employed at and near Harriseahead, about three miles from Bemersley. " Harriseahead had no means of grace, and the

---

* See the concluding chapter in B. Kirkman Gray's "A History of English Philanthropy."

inhabitants, chiefly colliers, appeared to be entirely destitute of religion, and much addicted to ungodliness. It was indeed reckoned a profane neighbourhood above most others." Hugh Bourne and Harriseahead! Here we have the man and the locality which for seven years to come concern us. Meanwhile from Harriseahead as our viewpoint we can glance at the moral condition of some other districts in the first third of the last century.

Morals and Manners in the Black Country, Holderness and Derby.—What we know as "the Black Country" was notorious for the rough and rude manners of the people. A stranger could hardly pass some of its villages without suffering annoyance or even maltreatment. It is no mere fable which avers that the fact of the passer-by being unknown was enough to raise the cry: "Heave half a brick at him!" or reason sufficient to move the dog-fancier to encourage his favourite bull terrier to try its teeth on the stranger's legs. The sports of the people were rough and brutal. The yearly "Wakes" of the North and the "Feasts" of the South were often times of excess and violence, leaving blood and broken heads as their souvenirs. No wonder that the Camp Meetings were so frequently set in array "to counteract the evils of the wake." In the purely agricultural district of HOLDERNESS, in the East Riding of Yorkshire, it was an immemorial custom for a football match to be played between the rival villages of Hedon and Preston, on Maudlin, that is, Magdalene Sunday.

The two villages formed the respective goals, and the aim of the players was to drive home the ball through the windows of the first public-house found unprotected by shutters. The ball was kicked hither and thither, amid the partisan cries of the bystanders—women as well as men—and the oaths and yells of the combatants, many of whom suffered severely in bruised flesh and broken bones because some of the players tipped their boots with hard leather or steel to make their kicks more telling. Strong drink flowed freely. The whole country was alive with excitement and vocal with partisan cries. Preston Church has been known to empty as the ball drew near ; and the parson after finishing his service would give a largess of drink to the winners. It was on Maudlin Sunday that the first Camp Meeting was held at Preston, and, after a few anniversaries of the day had passed over, the unseemly and brutalising sport had ceased to be. But we are not sure that enlightened DERBY would not have borne away the palm from benighted Preston-in-Holderness. It was the ancient custom for a football match to be played through the streets of Derby on Shrove Tuesday and Ash Wednesday. The event threw the whole town into confusion and was more like a battle than a game—a battle in which men were left " bruised, blinded and bleeding." The year 1846 saw the suppression of the unseemly saturnalia ; but it needed a posse of special constables and a troop of dragoons to do it.

A Time of War.—We begin this book, as we shall have to end it, with War, and there are many points of similarity between the two periods that could be pointed out. Some of the years of this period—notably 1811–14—will ever be famous in the military annals of Great Britain. Our missionaries would frequently be reminded by what they saw and heard that England was engaged in a terrible and exhausting struggle. The stage-coach drives through the village. The guard blows his horn and announces the latest victory amid loud huzzaings. Clashing bells celebrate the event. At nightfall the flaring tar-barrel lights the missionary to his billet. Often does. he come in contact with widows and orphans the war has made. As he takes his stand at market-cross or on village green, broken and disabled soldiers, or discharged veterans who had fought in the Peninsula or at Waterloo, are found among his hearers. As we follow our narrative let us be aware of these things, though they may be in the dim background.

Taxation and Food Scarcity.—The great Napoleonic War brought with it as its penalties, heavy taxation and, after the general peace, a terrible reaction. Thousands of disbanded soldiers were thrown on the labour-market. To add to the misery of the times a succession of bad harvests raised corn to famine prices. 1800 was known as "the dear year." You have a picture of those starving times in the early part of " John Halifax, Gentleman." Thomas Cooper in his autobiography tells us of the privations his mother and he endured at Gainsborough in the winter of 1813–14. " At one time," he says, " wheaten flour rose to six shillings per stone, and we had to live on barley-cakes, which brought on a burning, gnawing pain at the stomach. For two seasons the corn was spoiled in the fields with wet; and when the winter came we could scoop out the middle of the soft distasteful loaf; and to eat it brought on sickness. Meat was so dear that my mother could not buy it; and often our dinner consisted of potatoes only." 1818 has been described as the darkest period in the history of the century. The harvest of 1817 had been bad beyond all precedent. The inflation of the war-time had collapsed like a burst bladder. Trade was depressed. The Industrial Revolution was getting the upper hand and like a Juggernaut crushing those who stood in its way. Many forms of industry were thrown out of gear by the introduction of machinery and labour-saving appliances. Unsightly, barrack-like factories were rising on every hand, and the old, more leisurely days of domestic industries were soon to be things of the past. A great cry of distress went up from the starving victims of this inevitable transition from hand to machine which was to produce such wealth and work such untold suffering.

Discontent and Violence: the Luddites and the Levellers.—As was natural, misery bred discontent; and discontent resorted to violent measures as a remedy. The new machinery was regarded as *the* enemy. In 1811 the manufacturing districts of the Midlands were greatly disturbed by the doings of the "Luddites," as they called themselves. Bands of exasperated, desperate men ravaged the country, destroying the hated machines and committing excesses of various kinds—intimidation, pillage, personal violence. In 1812 the disturbances extended into Lancashire, Cheshire and the West Riding of Yorkshire. In Charlotte Brontë's " Shirley," readers will find the state of things which obtained in the West Riding graphically described. Coincidences of time and place meet us here ; for Luddism began at Nottingham in the same year in which Primitive Methodism began at Tunstall ; and while this *sabotage* was going on, and largely within the same area, Primitive Methodism was gathering and trying its new-born strength to cope with the spirit of disaffection and lawlessness that was abroad. But it strove to cope with it in a very different fashion from the Government which bore with a heavy hand on the disturbers of the public peace. How merciless was the action of the authorities may be learned from our histories, when they tell us that "no less than seventeen men were condemned to death, and executed in the courtyard of the castle at York at one time, for crimes connected with these disturbances."

The traditions and methods of the Luddites were handed on to the " Levellers." But there was a difference between them : the Levellers nursed a bitterer spirit and an animus more distinctly political. They cherished subversive designs and, in many cases, went a long way to justify their name. The Government was not scrupulous ; it sought to counterwork the designs of the Levellers by an odious system of espionage. Seven men were hanged at Leicester for destroying machinery to the value of £7,500 at Loughborough.   That was a short time before the Primitive Methodists gained a footing in the latter town.   It was with the Levellers, more than with the Luddites, our Church was brought into contact, as the dates of the great Midland revival show.   That the Levellers and Primitive Methodists were something more than contemporaries but occasionally crossed each other's path is proved by the well authenticated story told by George Herod, the substance of which we give in our own words.

In a village eight miles south-east of Leicester—Countesthorpe—arms were stored and nightly drillings went on.   Work was neglected until many stood on the verge of starvation.   In anticipation of a General Rising, timed to take place on June 9th, 1817, which was to usher in the era of lawlessness, a man took his revenge on one who had wronged him by maiming his sheep.   While the sheepmaimer was awaiting the sentence of death, his brother resolved to waylay the principal witness against the condemned man.   But before he could effect his purpose a " Ranter " preacher entered the village.   The would-be assassin, along with a number of his fellow-Levellers, was seized with conviction.   In the absence of the missionary he convened a meeting for prayer in his father's house ; but there was no one present who could lead the devotions.   They could sing, but they could not pray.   So, bethinking him, he took a book of family devotions out of the closet and himself undertook

the duty of prayer-leader ; and the singing and
the praying by book went on by turns. For many
years that man, rescued from the dominion of evil
passions, maintained a consistent Christian course ;
and the barn which had served as an armoury for
the Levellers was turned into the preaching room
at Countesthorpe.

England from 1819 to 1832.—Viewed in relation
to the social condition of England 1819 and 1820
are important dates. In the former year occurred
the " battle " of Peterloo ; in the latter the Cato
Street conspiracy, for which Thistlewood and his
starving companions were hanged. With the close
of the first two decades of the century the old evil
days seemed to have passed. Revived trade,
better harvests, brightened the face of things.
The improvement lasted until 1825–6, when a
financial crash came in which both Sir Walter Scott
and young Cobden were sufferers. On the heels
of this financial crash followed disaster and widespread misery, destined, however, to be the gloomy
precursors of the reform of 1832. Perhaps enough
has been said to prove that England in the first third
of the last century stood much in need of earnest
evangelism. The glorious work done by the
Evangelical Revival in the preceding century
needed to be done over again in a much more populous
England. The gospel with its regenerative, con-
solatory and restraining power needed to be brought
to men in such a way as to rouse them from their
absorption in secular pursuits. And yet the Churches

of the land too largely neglected home evangelisation. They were either unequal to the task or unmindful of it.   In their enthusiasm for the heathen abroad, they overlooked the semi-heathen at their own doors.   Their eyes were turned to lands beyond the seas, so that the benighted condition of the lapsed and lapsing masses of their own countrymen was temporarily forgotten.   Things may be bad enough now, but they were immeasurably worse then. Does not the contrast between *then* and *now* almost compel the inference that some such earnest evangelism as was called for has, in the Providence of God, been supplied ?   How far, and in what ways, Primitive Methodism may claim to have supplied that lack by going down amongst the neglected who were " perishing for lack of know-ledge "—let the reader decide for himself after he has read these pages.

CHAPTER II.

The Well-head of Primitive Methodism.

"It is possible that the 'wisdom of a poor man' may start a proposal which may 'save a city'—serve a nation! A single hair, applied to a flyer that has other wheels depending on it, may eradicate an oak, or pull down a house."

COTTON MATHER, D.D.

I. THE REAL BEGINNING.

The True Starting-point of Primitive Methodism.— In the working dictionary that lies to hand on our table "Primitive Methodist" happens to be immediately followed by the word "Primordial," which is defined as "first of all, first in order; original; first principle or element." Now it is just the *primordia* of Primitive Methodism—the beginnings of its beginning—we are in search of. Or, if we prefer a concrete figure, if we are looking for the first trickle from the well-spring which, as it makes its way downwards, fed from other sources, will at last become the broad, navigable river—then we must look to Hugh Bourne at Harriseahead on December 25th, 1800. The greatest transactions begin in the minds of men. The finest issues proceed out of the heart: and Hugh Bourne "moved with compassion" as he beheld the morally destitute condition of the people around him, is the well-head we wanted to find. It was the perception of the urgent need for evangelisation that was the first quickening impulse of our Connexional life, when as yet there was no Connexion or the semblance or dream of one. We began in Conversation-preaching ; and we may be glad we began in that way. Conversation-preaching was before the Camp Meeting in time ; and it is before it in significance. Hugh Bourne's plain direct dealing with his cousin that Christmas Day takes us back to the calling of the first disciples ; to Christ's sermon " to a congregation of one " at the well ; to Philip sitting with the eunuch in his chariot preaching Christ to him. We here get back to first principles, and we shall have to get back to them on a wide scale and in a practical way before the world is to be converted.

The Christmas Conversation-Sermon.—At Harriseahead, " Hugh Bourne," he tells us, " endeavoured to promote religion there, and on the 24th and 25th of December, 1800, he prevailed with a collier, named Daniel Shubotham, at Harriseahead, fully to set out for heaven." Here we have the fact baldly stated ; but in his Journal he wrote an account while the impression of what had taken place was still fresh :—

" Last night I lay down in sorrow, and this morning I arose in sorrow ; the main cause of my grief was my kinsman not being born again of God. My natural timidity pressed upon me, so that to me it was a task to go ; but my mouth had been opened before the Lord, and to have drawn back would have been awful. So off I set, taking with me a book written by R. Barclay, the Quaker ; and I took the written account of my own conversion and experience. It was a sorrowful journey ; but I found Daniel waiting for me, so my introduction was easy. Having never prayed in public, and judging myself not capable of it, I did not pray with the family ; but, knowing him to be hindered by an erroneous notion, read him a piece out of Barclay, with which he declared himself satisfied ; so the way was open. Next followed a little general conversation. I then rose up to go, requesting him to accompany me a little way. I was full of sorrow, but so soon as we were in a suitable place, I set-to preaching the Gospel to him with all my might, taking up John xiv. 21, where the words of Jesus Christ are : ' I will love him and will manifest Myself to him.' At parting I put into his hands the full account of my own conversion and experience. I then took leave ; but parted from him in sorrow, fearing he did not take sufficient notice, and I passed the day in sorrow. But God's thoughts were not as my thoughts, for Daniel afterwards told me, that when I was talking to him that morning every word went through him."

The Harriseahead Period, 1801-1807.—" Nearly at the same time," continues Hugh Bourne, " another collier, named Matthias Bayley was, by other means, brought in the way of heaven. These men were very earnest, and there was soon a considerable awakening. A work of religion, usually called a ' revival,' took place . . . and there was a great reformation in the neighbourhood." We do not forget that the religious society that was now formed at Harriseahead was a Methodist society, though of the Revivalistic type. The only reason, therefore, we have for annexing any incidents belonging these years is derived from their causal relation to what will follow. For Hugh Bourne these years were a period of discipline and training. Even on this stony, moorland edge of North Staffordshire, his talent for organising and leadership

already found some scope. He became immersed
in chapel-building, for which he gave timber, supervision and financial assistance. He learnt much,
and he taught much. For a year he taught a school
in the new chapel, both on the week-day and—
what is interesting to note—on the Sunday. Meanwhile he was teaching himself Greek and Hebrew,
and evidently shorthand too. He learned to pray
and speak in public, though when he made his
first attempt to preach in the open air it was with
his hand before his face—a characteristic attitude
he never lost. He gained experience of class-meetings
and of revivals with which Harriseahead was
favoured—revivals which helped still further to
" moralise " the district and spread through the
Burslem Circuit. For us this period is also interesting
as that in which the idea of a Camp Meeting had
its origin and, ultimately, its realisation. The first
rough idea of a camp meeting was thrown out
by Daniel Shubotham in the promise : " You shall
have a day's praying on Mow, and then you'll be
satisfied." But this rudimentary idea took more
definite shape through the accounts of the American
Camp Meetings that began to appear in the " Methodist Magazine." It was, unquestionably, the visit of
Lorenzo Dow to these parts, and especially his visit
to Harriseahead, which proved the decisive factor.
The literature on the subject Dow circulated was
eagerly read. The upshot was that a Camp Meeting
on Mow Cop was arranged to be held on May 31st,
1807. This may be said to be Daniel Shubotham's
Camp Meeting ; for Hugh Bourne had already

decided in his own mind to hold one at Norton on August 23rd. But Daniel in his impulsive way said, " This is the Camp Meeting ! " and nothing loath, Hugh Bourne acquiesced, and took the leading part in preparing for it.

II. THE METHODIST CAMP-MEETINGERS.

" Whenever the weather will permit, go out in God's name into the most public places, and call all to repent and believe the Gospel : every Sunday, in particular ; especially where there are old Societies, lest they settle on their lees."

JOHN WESLEY, *Minutes* of Conference, 1744.

First Mow Cop Camp Meeting, May 31st, 1807.— Elsewhere we have told at large the story of Mow Cop Camp Meeting and need not go over the familiar story once more. It will suffice if we borrow and pass on the glowing sentences from William Clowes' Journal in which he recalls the scenes and recovers the impressions of that high day.

" The first day's praying on Mow-hill presented at this period a most magnificent and sublime spectacle. Four preachers simultaneously crying to sinners to flee from the wrath to come ; thousands listening, affected by ' thoughts that breathe and words that burn ' ; many in deep distress, and others pleading with Heaven on their behalf; some praising God aloud for the great things which were brought to pass ; whilst others were rejoicing in the testimony which they had received, that their sins, which were many, had been all forgiven. The Camp Meeting continued full of glory and converting power. About four o'clock in the afternoon the number of people was prodigiously large ; but after this time many began to move off the ground and to retire homewards ; yet the power of the Highest continued with undiminished force and effect until the very last. Towards the conclusion the services were principally carried on by praying companies, and at the close, which took place about half-past eight o'clock in the evening, several souls were set at liberty. At the termination of this memorable day I felt excessively exhausted, as I had laboured from the commencement of the meeting in the morning until eight o'clock in the evening with very little cessation; but the glory that filled my soul on that day far exceeds my powers of description to explain. Much of the good wrought at this great meeting remains; but the full amount of that good, eternity alone will develop to the myriads of the angelic and sainted inhabitants, who will everlastingly laud the Eternal Majesty on account of the day's praying on Mow-hill."

Readers can hardly fail to detect the lyrical note to which Clowes' prose has attained in his last sentence as he thinks back to this "day of grace."

Norton the Critical and Decisive Camp Meeting, August 23–5, 1807.—The importance of the Norton-le-Moors Camp Meeting rests in the fact that it was held after the Methodist Conference had given its veto against Camp Meetings. The Conference asked :—

Q. " What is the judgment of the Conference concerning what are called Camp Meetings ? "

A. " In our judgment that, even supposing such means be allowable in America, they are highly improper in England, and likely to be of considerable mischief; and we disclaim all connection with them."

Prior to the passing and promulgation of this edict, arrangements had been made to hold a Camp Meeting at Norton to counteract the evils of the Wake. Burslem Circuit was the storm-centre of the new movement. The projected Camp Meeting would supply a test-case. Armed with the Conference pronouncement the ministers of the Circuit took action. The officials were gathered together and asked to do as the Conference bade them—" disclaim all connection with Camp Meetings." Some who had taken an active part in the two " loathly allowed " Camp Meetings previously held were intimidated. Daniel Shubotham (Shufflebottom) was true to his real name. Even James Bourne for a time hesitated ; but finally resolved to stand by his brother whatever might be the consequences. But, anxious as he was, Hugh Bourne did not flinch ; and James Nixon and Thomas Cotton remained firm. The fateful day came. At first the outlook was depressing, mainly because of the shortage of labourers. On the Monday the face of things brightened. Dr. Paul Johnson had been impressed to travel all the way from Ireland to render help, and his unexpected appearance on the Camp-ground put fresh courage into the hearts of the leaders. It must not be forgotten that those who organised the first and second Camp Meetings were Methodists and that the meetings were held in the, name of Methodism. Even so regarded they were impressive demonstrations of the prevalence at the time of what was known as " Revivalism," and of the widespread desire to do more than was being done by the Churches to lay hold of the neglected classes. This " Revivalism " took various forms in different localities and was known by various names. There were " Tent Methodists " at Bristol, " Band Room Methodists " in Manchester, " Quaker

C

Methodists " (afterwards known as "Independent Methodists ") at Warrington. In Leeds, Hull, Bristol, Sheffield, Nottingham and other large towns there were many who sympathised with Methodism of this more fervid type, and who sought to revive the spirit and the methods of " old " or " primitive " Methodism. There were even some prominent ministers who had strong Revivalistic tendencies as we know from the " Life " of William Bramwell and others. On the other hand it was eyed askance and with disfavour by many men of weight and influence. To them, in the anxious years that followed the death of John Wesley, 1791, it seemed clear that the first charge was to safe-guard and consolidate the Methodism of which they were in trust. The particular form Hugh Bourne's " Revivalism " took on was, getting back to the open-air preaching of Wesley and Whitefield. But he was no servile imitator of their methods. He was firmly convinced that a modification of the old field-preaching could still be made effective in reaching the class that had seemed unreachable by the ordinary agencies. There must be more preachers than one, and none must be " a long preacher," as the familar phrase went. Above all, the preaching must be well mixed with prayer. So there must be praying-circles, temporary or permanent—the latter by preference. These were the ideas Hugh Bourne strove to embody. He organised and successfully carried through the famous first Camp Meeting of May 31st, and the elaborately-staged and legally-threatened Camp

Meeting of July 19th. The Revivalists of all shades rallied to the support of this novel form of propagandism. But these two impressive gatherings might have ended in little but a memory had the presiding genius of Camp Meetings not had an inflexible will as well as ideas and enthusiasm. At Norton Hugh Bourne was on his trial, just as the Camp Meeting movement itself was ; and the trial was successfully passed for both. Mow Cop's fame is assured. The sentiment of our Church has enwrapped its " bleak and frowning summit " as with a halo. Tradition has it in safe keeping. At the same time we see distinctly now that, historically, Norton overtops the hill of Mow. Its significance lies in the fact that by it the perpetuity of the Camp Meeting movement on English ground was assured. The Camp Meeting was fashioned to be no mere evangelistic toy, but to be a well-tempered and serviceable weapon for aggressive use. It had come to stay. Until Norton Camp Meeting was over this could not have been said.

III. THE CAMP MEETING METHODISTS.

Hugh Bourne is " put out " of the Methodist Society, June 27th, 1808.—In establishing Camp Meetings Hugh Bourne disestablished himself. Ten months after Norton Wake Camp Meeting he was summarily dealt with by the Burslem quarterly meeting. In his absence, unnotified of any charge hanging over him, he was dismembered. It is true he was not either a recognised leader or local preacher ;

but he was a trustee, and as such, one thinks, might have had opportunity to answer for himself. The charge preferred against him was non-attendance at his class ; but the real reason of his expulsion was afterwards stated in a private conversation which the superintendent had with Hugh Bourne. " Why did you put me out ? " The frank answer was, " Because you have a tendency to set up other than the ordinary worship." The blow was not unexpected ; before it fell he had reckoned with it. He paid his arrears of class-money and went on with his evangelistic work. He did not pose as a martyr ; much less did he seek to foment bitter feeling or create division. For close upon two years we see him still a Methodist, but *unattached*.

James Crawfoot enters into the Work, November 1809.—There was another man smarting at this time from the action of an official meeting. This was James Crawfoot, the head of the " Forest," or " Magic Methodists of Delamere Forest." Crawfoot had lost his position as a Methodist local preacher for preaching on an emergency for the Quaker Methodists in Friars' Green Chapel, Warrington, in 1807. Unchurched, he still went on holding meetings in his own peculiar fashion. The fame of these meetings had spread into Staffordshire. It was reported that Crawfoot's disciples talked much of " exercising faith in silence," and went into visions and trances. The news drew Hugh Bourne to the Forest. In 1807, accompanied by William Clowes, he attended one of the monthly meetings in

Crawfoot's house. Now Crawfoot was a rustic mystic, and his influence on Bourne and Clowes, and through them on the Connexion, was considerable. He thought and spoke much on the meaning of spiritual conflicts, the mystery of faith, and the way of bringing power to bear on men. In November 1809, the Bourne brothers agreed to pay Crawfoot ten shillings a week that he might devote himself to evangelistic work. His instructions were : to labour on the Cheshire and Staffordshire sides on alternate fortnights, and to advise his converts to join the denominations to which they were most inclined. In 1813 James Crawfoot ceased to be a travelling preacher ; but, though his labours had no long continuance, they lasted long enough to entitle him to be regarded as one of the makers of Primitive Methodism. The " Old Man of the Forest " had no turn for practical affairs, but when he spoke on deep spiritual things men listened as if he had been something of an oracle or prophet of God.

CHAPTER III.

The Start of Primitive Methodism and Its Course to 1819.

" Large streams from little fountains flow,
Tall oaks from little acorns grow."

I.   THE CAMP MEETING METHODISTS
(continued).

Hugh Bourne becomes the head of the Camp Meeting Methodists, May 1810.—For two years Hugh Bourne and his helpers clung to the skirts of the Old Body, just as the latter had clung to the skirts of the Established Church. We know in what a step-motherly way the early Methodists were treated ; they got more cuffs than caresses. So history repeated itself in 1809–10. It was impossible things could remain on this unsatisfactory footing for any length of time. The refusal of the Burslem Circuit authorities to take over the Standley society of ten members raised by the Bournes and their helpers, except on the condition that the society would have nothing more to do with the Camp Meetingers, brought things to a head. The Standley society declined to give the required undertaking, and so the onus of decision now lay with Hugh Bourne and his followers. They were thus faced with a double responsibility : not only had they to get men converted, but to look after them when they were converted. They shouldered the responsibility. So it was that, as by the simple pull of a lever, the unattached Camp Meeting Methodists now became a small but distinct community. Had an understanding of this kind been arrived at two years earlier, the contribution of the Camp Meeting Methodists towards the formation of the Primitive Methodist Connexion in 1811 would have been much larger than it was. What was left them to give was the mere salvage of what they had won and parted with.

II. William Clowes and the "Clowesites."

William Clowes' Conversion (1805).—However strong may be the temptation to dwell on the life William Clowes lived when he was in "the wild olive tree which is wild by nature" we must forbear, and be content to start with the great experience which came to him on January 20th, 1805, when he had nearly completed his twenty-fifth year. He was one of the many converts of the great Revival which, beginning at Harriseahead, spread through the whole of the Burslem Circuit. James Nixon, "precious" Thomas Woodnorth, William Morris, Samuel Barber (the son of Dr. Samuel Johnson's coloured confidential servant) were all arrested and swept into the Church in this same great Revival of 1805. Clowes' conversion was catastrophic; nor could it well have been anything else, considering the man and the life he had led. The powers of hell "gat hold upon him." His soul was shaken and torn as by some terrible convulsion. But, like Paul, he obtained mercy ; and the sense of that mercy was like the shining of the sun on a renewed world. His change and profiting soon appeared to all. Some, who in knowing fashion predicted that a few weeks or months at most would see him back in his old haunts and amongst his old companions in the tavern and ball-room, were grievously out in their reckoning. Clowes meant business—and heavenly business—and he put all his capital and every ounce of his energy into it. So rapid was his advance in the divine life that Hugh Bourne wondered and was emulous and almost envious of the progress he was making. " He grows up into God at a very great rate," he muses ; and again, " Such a man I scarcely ever met with. O God, that Thou wouldst make me like him ! " Vain wish, if it meant that the vessels should be of like pattern ! Better as it was ! Both vessels were made " meet for the Master's use " ; but the vessels were as different from each other as difference could be, and so remained to the end. It is important to recognise that Clowes was never a Camp Meeting Methodist in the sense Hugh Bourne was one. He believed in the Camp Meeting as a useful auxiliary ; but there never was danger of its becoming an obsession with him. He threw himself with ardour into the first Mow Camp Meeting and was present at the second ; but Norton did not see his face or hear his voice. As we read the facts, the actual, concrete Methodism of the time was much more to him than it ever was to Hugh Bourne.

William Clowes' Expulsion, September 1810.—
William Clowes was converted in an old-time
Revival, the note of which was full salvation, and
it is clear that his revivalistic sympathies were
deepened by reflection and his own evangelistic
experiences. So it was that, though his name had
stood on the Burslem plan since November 1809, he
felt drawn by strong impulse as well as friendship to
take a prominent part in the Ramsor Camp Meeting
of June 3rd, 1810. This was for Clowes the guillotine
Camp Meeting ; it cut him off from the Old Body.
This act, instead of silencing him, served only to un-
loose his tongue, and he became increasingly popular.
Then in September his ticket of membership was
withheld on the express ground of his participation
in Camp Meetings. Events now followed thick
and fast. The greater number of Clowes' members
were drawn after him by the unexerted but attractive
force of his personality. Messrs. Nixon, Woodnorth, Morris and Barber were either " dealt with "
by the authorities or showed their sympathy with
Clowes by sharing his fortunes. The unchurched
found a home in the kitchen of Mr. Smith, where
for two years a meeting for prayer and preaching
had been held every Friday night. These services
were the indirect outcome of Norton Camp Meeting
and were Revivalistic and irregular (that is unofficial)
in character. In December 1810, Messrs. Nixon and
Woodnorth guaranteed William Clowes ten shillings
a week that he might give himself more fully to
missionary labours. These labours now took a
wider range, and the Church in the kitchen soon

became the nucleus of a Circuit, the adherents of the new cause being everywhere known as "Clowesites." In the Methodist society at Tunstall discipline still went on and was exercised rather wildly. Mr. James Steele was ousted from the superintendency of the Sunday School, and the leadership of two classes was taken from him. Here agáin, a number of members, teachers and scholars refused to be parted from one whom they had come to respect and love. After due consideration Mr. Steele cast in his lot with the Clowesites. As the kitchen was now too small for the augmented congregation, a remove was made to Mr. Boden's warehouse, and preparations began for the building of a chapel which was opened on July 13th, 1811. Its builders could not see far before them, so as thrifty men they saw to it that the chapel could easily be converted into four dwelling-houses. The Bourne brothers were sole trustees until 1821 of this first Tunstall chapel.

The Importance of the Clowesite Factor.—Was there ever a band of men familiarly known to their contemporaries as "Clowesites"? This is not the trivial question it seems: a good deal depends on the answer given to it. There is abundant evidence that the name "Clowesites" survived in local use many years. It had currency in Cheshire, as we learn from Thomas Bateman's Diary. John Flesher, too, may be cited as a witness on the same side. Writing in 1843, he recalls how, on his first visit to Staffordshire twelve years before, he was everywhere hearing people speak of "Clowes' Chapel" and of the "Clowesites." Commenting on this he writes : "If the facts of the case be as the people speak of them, the History of Primitive Methodism, as published, must be defective, inasmuch as Clowes is comparatively hidden, whereas he ought to be brought before the public as one of the founders of the Connexion, if not the founder. To say the least of the affair, it is deserving of inquiry, and I think a History of the Connexion ought to be written which will place the rise of the Connexion on a legitimate basis." These are weighty words as coming from John Flesher. True, the strictures on the first History we would fain believe do not apply with the same force to the subsequent ones ; but it is doubtful whether, even yet, we have agreement as to the only standpoint for gaining a true perspective of our history. Mr. Flesher's words give rise to reflections which can rest only in the recognition that the founders of the two sections which combined to form Primitive Methodism have equal claims to be adjudged *our* founders. The union of the two sections was an unmixed good, since it ensured that Primitive Methodism was something more than a Camp Meeting movement. If it had not been more than that then, when the historical decline of Camp Meetings came, as eventually it did, the *raison d'être* of Primitive Methodism would also have gone. Who will be forward to take up such a position ?

A New Denomination is Born, May 1811.—When
in May 1811, like came to like and the Camp Meeting
Methodists and the Clowesites agreed to unite their
fortunes and make common cause, a new denomination was born.   The printed ticket of membership
was the first visible symbol of corporate life.
" Prior to that time," says Hugh Bourne, " the
Connexion, being begun in the order of Divine
providence, was held together by a zeal for the
Lord of Hosts."   Beyond the single date " May
1811 " the ticket had on it only the significant
text, " But we desire to hear of thee what thou
thinkest ; but as concerning this sect it is everywhere
spoken against."   Then on May 26th the brethren,
assembled in Mr. Smith's kitchen, did something
towards giving the new denomination its rudimentary
organisation.   They steered clear of the threatening
rock of Free Gospelism in affirming that they who
are set apart to preach the Gospel, should live
by the Gospel ; and that the two travelling preachers,
James Crawfoot and William Clowes, should be
maintained by the contributions of the joint
societies ; but Hugh Bourne, for the time being,
declined to benefit by the principle affirmed.   He
would bear his own charges ; and William Alcock,
who was largely given up to the work, was of the
same mind.   Finally, as moneys would have to be
received and disbursed, the brethren appointed
James Steele Circuit Steward.

The Name " Primitive Methodist " taken, February
1812.—In Hugh Bourne's Journal we have an

entry signifying by its bolder script his sense of the importance of the record :—" Thursday, February 13th, 1812, we called a meeting and made plans for the next quarter, and made some other regulations : in particular, we took the name of THE SOCIETY OF THE PRIMITIVE METHODISTS." To us the adoption of our legal, denominational name was the most memorable item of business transacted on that St. Valentine's eve of 1812. Yet we are assured by Mr. Petty, on the testimony of Hugh Bourne himself, that the name was decided upon at the fag-end of a long business session when Hugh Bourne, jaded by what he had gone through, was overcome by drowsiness. When he came to himself the thing was done ; the christening was over. To James Crawfoot was undoubtedly due the suggestion of the name, and probably his advocacy led to its adoption. Once again he would tell the story of John Wesley's farewell address to the preachers of Chester Circuit in 1790—the story Crawfoot related when vindicating his action in preaching for the Quaker Methodists. When brought to book for this he had applied the story in the final words : " Mr. Chairman, if you have deviated from the old usages I have not ; I still remain a *primitive* Methodist." Now, Crawfoot would contend, the time had come for turning the small " p " into a capital letter, and for making Primitive Methodist a title descriptive of the ideal the denomination would ever set before it. It was done : Crawfoot prevailed. The name seemed predestined and inevitable. It was appropriate and could be historically justified.

A Threatening Political Danger Averted, 1811–12.— If the ticket bearing the date May 1811 was as a certificate of birth, then Lord Sidmouth's abortive Bill of May 9th and 21st was a cute and determined effort " to seek the young child's life." Had the Bill brought in passed into an Act, Methodism would have been vitally hurt and Primitive Methodism would have been strangled in its cradle. Itinerating evangelists—who according to the noble lord's elegant phraseology, mostly consisted of " cobblers, tailors, pig-drivers and chimney-sweeps "—would have found their occupation gone. But the Bill roused such antagonism throughout the country that it never became an Act. Three days after it was thrown out, the Protestant Society for the Protection of Religious Liberty was founded, and this Society worked so effectually that in July 1812 the obnoxious Quakers' Oaths, the Conventicle, and the Five Mile Acts were repealed. Thomas Russell and other of our missionaries had abundant reason to bless the Protestant Society and its devoted Secretary John Wilkes, M.P., who was to be our legal adviser in preparing the Deed Poll.

III.—A PAUSE FOLLOWED BY A SWIFT ADVANCE, 1811–19

" Why satest thou among the sheep-folds
To hear the pipings for the flocks ? "
JUDGES V. 16.

" But zeal and enterprise, as well as caution and prudence, are requisite for the well-being of Christian societies, as well as for the evangelisation of the world."
REV. JOHN PETTY.

" The Tunstall Non-Mission Law " and What it Meant.—As is shown by the incontestable evidence of figures, the Connexion did not make any considerable advance, either geographical or numerical, for eight years. After 1811, when the membership stood at two hundred, no returns were given until the first Conference of 1820. The report then given was as follows : eight circuits ; forty-eight travelling preachers ; 277 local preachers and 7,842 members, half of whom Mr. Petty finds reason to believe had been added during the preceding year. An average yearly addition of 490 to the membership in the eight successive years from 1811 to 1819 does not afford much ground for Connexional jubilation. What was wrong ? Where shall we find the seat of the trouble ? Hugh Bourne does not mince matters. He affirms—often and at length— the mistaken cry was raised : " For the present let Consolidation be our main business, and not Extension. That will come all in good time. Meanwhile we shall be gainers in the end by giving ourselves to the building up of our societies." The cry was plausible but unsound ; for the long history of the Church shows that she progresses by the joint action of the two things the cry sundered. Extension and Consolidation must go on together. There must be a double movement, or the Church will fare like the bird which attempts to fly with a broken wing.

John Benton Breaks the Non-Mission Law, 1812– 16.—If this mistaken policy were more than an

understanding and actually got itself shaped into
a "law," there were those who with great satisfaction broke it forthwith ; and it was well they did.
Such free-lances—and who shall say they were not
the true succession ?—were John Benton, John
Wedgewood and Eleazar Hathorn. Benton had
pleaded at the Quarterly Meeting that " Primitive
Methodism should be allowed to go through the
land as it was raised up to do." When his pleading was set aside he refused his plan, and when it
was sent after him he sent it back again enriched
with a stanza of his own composing :

> " A plan from God I have to mind,
> A better plan I cannot find.
> If *you* can, pray let me know,
> And round the Circuit I will go."

He adapted Lorenzo Dow's Hymn Book to his
use, got a thousand copies printed, and then set
off to mission on his own account. Benton succeeded in carving out a Circuit on the East Staffordshire border and handed it over to Hugh Bourne
to organise and look after—October 1814. Thence,
with the help of Eleazar, Hathorn (who had taken
part in the first Camp Meeting on Mow) he went
evangelising among the Derbyshire villages, where
John Ride and John Harrison were won for the
Connexion. Hugh Bourne, well pleased at the way
things were moving in these parts, began a Tract
Mission, called Mary Hawksley into the work and
became responsible for her modest salary, and
busied himself in establishing and equipping Sunday

Schools. An important advance was made when Benton, with his band of village supporters, missioned Belper. This town was our Antioch; for a foolish man resident there dubbed us " Ranters," and the ugly name stuck to us like a burr for half a century. Here, Sarah Kirkland of Mercaston comes on the scene. She was prevailed upon to preach in Derby, and from that time the denomination gained a sure footing in this important county town. Next, at the solicitation and with the help of Robert Winfield of Ambaston, a Methodist local preacher of Revivalistic sympathies, she introduced Primitive Methodism into Nottingham at the Christmastide of 1815. Soon the factory on the Broad Marsh was acquired and became the centre of a vigorous cause. A notable Camp Meeting at Mercaston—on the new model, plentifully intermixed with prayer—put new life into Hugh Bourne Benton went fresh from it all afire to resume his evangelistic work. When in 1816 Derby was made the head of the second Circuit in the Connexion, a victory was won by the enlargers over the consolidators! On no other terms than entire independence of Tunstall and its Non-Mission Law was denominational homogeneity possible.

The Great Revival in the Midlands, 1816–18.— A great Camp Meeting in Nottingham Forest on Whit Sunday, 1816, said to be attended by twelve thousand people, ushered in the Great Revival. Four " Johns " were the chief agents in carrying on the work—Benton, Wedgewood, Heath and Halls-

D

worth; and, in 1818 John Harrison. Nor should
the great part taken in the Revival by Sarah Kirkland be overlooked. In 1816–17 the Revival was
mainly in Notts., with extensions into Lincolnshire.
Then it turned towards Leicestershire, and Loughborough was entered, to become in 1818 the third
Circuit in the Connexion, Nottingham by this time
having superseded Derby as the second Circuit.
Says Mr. Herod in his " Sketches " : " We consider that the Revival that took place in the counties
of Nottingham and Leicester in the years 1817 and
1818 was one of the most remarkable that was ever
experienced in the Primitive Methodist Connexion.
. . . In about one year and nine months not less
than seventy-five towns and villages were missioned,
and not less than seventy-five local preachers were
raised up." Some of these entered the ministry and
in due time became enlargers of the Connexion,
notably Messrs. King, the three Garner brothers,
Bonser, Moss, Oscroft, Charlton and Herod himself.
At this time William Clowes was the leading preacher
in the Tunstall Circuit, but the imprisonment of
Wedgewood at Grantham in 1817 liberated him
for a time. Never, surely, was more work crowded
into a brief fortnight. He was brought in contact
with the Revival and reacted upon it in such a way
as to give it increased impetus. He paid a second
visit to the Revival area in 1818, making excursions
also into Rutland and Lincolnshire. The same year
Lorenzo Dow with Dorothy Ripley went over the
track of the Revival, beginning at Nottingham and
ending at Barlestone.

Hull is Reached, 1819.—We entered Hull at the invitation of Mrs. Woolhouse and a group of persons whom we may regard as Methodist " Revivalists." R. Winfield had been appointed missioner, but he threw up the appointment in a pique and withdrew to found the " Revivalists," a community which lingered for a few years in the Midlands. Who was to take his place ? Crawfoot had retired ; nor was John Benton available. He had seriously injured his larynx at the " Panic " Camp Meeting of Round Hill, May 1816. At this conjuncture Nottingham Circuit appealed by deputation to Tunstall, and William Clowes was chosen for the important mission. He entered Hull, the scene of his former frolics and escapades, and made his way to the Woolhouses, where he was made welcome and greatly encouraged by the consecration prayer of John Oxtoby. In Hull and Holderness—once " reckoned a most benighted part "—the work spread rapidly. John Harrison and Sarah Kirkland (now Mrs. Harrison) were added as second and third missionaries. Before the year 1819 ended Mill Street Chapel was built and Hull branch of Nottingham became an independent Circuit—the fourth. The holding at Nottingham of the Preparatory Meeting—which was in everything but the name the first Connexional Conference—brings a well-defined sub-period of our history to a close.

1819 *a Notable Year.*—The year of " Peterloo " is a convenient Connexional date-mark. 1819 was a point of convergence and radiation ; a year of endings and beginnings. As we have seen, it prepared the way for the first Conference ; it saw the issue of the first Connexional Magazines and opened a new and stirring chapter in Tunstall's missionary enterprise. It marked, too, the close of what we may call the campaign in the Trent valley with a view to its occupation. The head-waters of the Trent rise not far from Mow Cop, and by 1819 much of the country watered by that rivei and its affluents had been penetrated. This scrap of fact from the physical geography of our land may help to fix in our mind where Primitive Methodism began its course and where it had got to in 1819. It was cradled by the sources of the Trent and it was in the country drained by that river and its tributaries that it tried its first strength and won its first successes. Just as in the wondrous hydraulics of nature the water gathered on the slopes of Mow may now, after many a devious wandering, be passing Hull's Southend Pier on its way to the sea, so that cause which had its rise in these same distant Potteries, has at last, in the person of its accredited agent and in the marvellous providence of God, reached the self-same spot.

The Personality of William Clowes.—Can we in any measure recover the impression William Clowes made on his contemporaries ? If we can, now is the time to do it, when we find him in Hull, in the zenith of his powers and just about to begin the work of his life. We have elsewhere attempted the " featuring " of William Clowes and, as we see little to modify, we will borrow the sketch for our present use. William Clowes was richly dowered by nature. His form and countenance were prepossessing; his disposition frank and open. There was much about him of that "inexplicable and undeniable thing called charm." He had a vivid, magnetic personality which seemed as though it could focus itself in his eye and concentrate in his voice. With a steady glance he could, and often did, make the mocker and the would-be persecutor quail; and his voice, especially in its higher inflections, would thrill and search the soul, until, so long as it vibrated, such a man as C. C. M'Kechnie —whom one would have thought proof against all such influence—was fain to grasp the form on which he sat to keep himself from falling.

Church Organisation still in the Rudimentary Stage, 1811–19.—Our fathers did not greatly concern themselves with Church-mechanics in these early years. On the contrary, they seem rather to have shunned a form of activity which some find so fascinating. They were slow to move, and when they did take action they were pushed on by sheer necessity. Not till 1814 were Society Rules drawn up and printed, and then only under strong pressure from the Societies. What will appear stranger still to us, there was no superintendent preacher until the same year, by which time it had become plain to all that some one must be made responsible for the "cutting off of neglects." Of course the burden fell on Hugh Bourne, and he fulfilled the duties of his onerous office until the very close of 1818, when his health completely broke down under the strain—as well it might. We have only to think of it—one superintendent for three Circuits, with Societies in five counties, necessitating continuous journeys nearly always on foot ! Other examples of organisation improvised to meet a felt want we have in the institution of Circuit Committees and Circuit " branches." Of neither of these regulations could it be said that it was the result of mere theorising. As Hugh Bourne truly says of those early days : " Improvements scarcely ever took place except through individual enterprise or when called forth by gradual necessity."

CHAPTER IV.

The Geographical Extension of Primitive Methodism from 1819 to 1833.

" To plant successfully a religious thought or system requires more violent aggression than to conquer a nation."

Wanted : a Bird's-eye View of the Progress Made.— It will require some effort to secure it ; but we are not without hope that it may be done. The essential thing to notice is that in 1819 there was no formal allotment of territory to the tribes of our Israel. Each, according to its zeal and ability, was trying to conquer as much of the good land for itself as it could. It is no deliberate, combined effort, to carry through a carefully considered plan of operations drawn up by the " General Staff " we have to study. For the present we wish to learn *Where* Primitive Methodism had got to—how much of English or other ground it had covered—by 1833. *How* it got there ; by what means and methods, and at what cost, are questions which can best be answered when we have got the bird's-eye view we are looking for.

The Circuit still the Unit of Missionary Activity.— For some time to come our eye has to follow the

movements of the four primary Circuits—Tunstall,
Nottingham, Loughborough and Hull. These, and
not the Districts as such, were the centres of
aggressive life. In the natural order of things
Circuits multiplied fast and in their turn took part
in the aggressive work of these years. The picture
becomes increasingly complex ; so much so that
to put it into print in a book of this scale is beyond
the art of man and must not be attempted.
Fortunately, it is not needed now ; for, if details
are wanted they can readily be found in the larger
History of our Church, and in the number of excellent
monographs dealing with particular areas which
have been published of late years. What may
suffice in this section is, to give the gist of the
multitudinous facts implicated in the bald statement
that, by 1833, the four primary Circuits had grown
to one hundred and one, and that Primitive
Methodism had penetrated into most parts of
England, and had boldly set foot in the United States
as well as in Scotland, Ireland and North and South
Wales.

*Hull Circuit's Part in the Enlargement of the
Connexion.*—A line drawn straight across the
map from Goole near the estuary of the Humber to
the river Ribble would very fairly show, in the land
lying to the north of it, the main sphere of Hull's
missionary labours. There would have to be one
or two inclusions and exclusions to make it strictly
accurate. For one thing, that interesting corner
of north-east Lincolnshire, whence the Pilgrim

Fathers embarked, would have to be taken in ; for Barton-on-Humber was a Branch of Hull until 1853 and was included in Hull District until the comparatively recent formation of the Grimsby and Lincoln District. Halifax, though lying north of our line, would have to be excluded as deriving from Nottingham ; so, possibly, might Bacup. After these adjustments it may safely be said that what Primitive Methodism there may be in the country lying north of this horizontal line has been derived, immediately or mediately, from Hull as the dynamic centre. How much ground had been broken up in the short space of three years is told us by William Clowes :—

" Tuesday, December 3rd, 1822. I set out for Hull, 180 miles, to attend the Quarterly Meeting. The ground is all broken up between Hull and Carlisle. Where it will go to next I cannot tell. But, through the mercy of God, I can preach my way from Newcastle to Hull, night by night, without break at all ; and this I can do on ground I have missioned through and broken up myself. During this quarter the ground has been broken up from Newcastle to Carlisle. Our Circuit extends from Carlisle in Cumberland to Spurn Point in Holderness, an extent of more than two hundred miles. What is the breadth of the Circuit I cannot tell ; it branches off various ways. From Carlisle the work seems to be opening two ways : one to White-haven and the other to Gretna Green in Scotland."

On the wide tract of country thus indicated, men were now or soon afterwards won for the Connexion who were to render it effective service—future ministers, such as William Harland the school-master, William Howcroft the poetaster, John Nelson, after Hugh Bourne our first author of repute, the popular and facetious Henry Hebbron, and

William Dent the sound Methodist divine. Of leading laymen we recall the names of Thomas Dawson, John Reynard, J. Gordon Black, Henry Hesman, Thomas Waller, J. D. Muschamp, George Race and Richard Raine, whose clear voice was destined in the after days to be heard leading the songs of praise at many a famous Camp Meeting— these, and many more, of whom " the time would fail to tell," were laid hold of and began their life-long allegiance to the Connexion.

Undoubtedly the years 1819–24 must be regarded as the outstanding period of Hull's evangelistic efforts. During these five years, from Hull " the fruitful mother " there had been made seventeen Circuits, with an aggregate membership of 7,666. There still remained with the parent Circuit 3,772 members, which made the number raised by Hull for the Connexion 11,432. Even after this, fresh conquests in a distant field were won by Hull's leading missionary. We find three Cornish Circuits —Redruth, St. Austell and St. Ives included within the freshly-formed Brinkworth District at the end of our period. This corner of the land had been taken possession of by Hull Circuit. We entered Cornwall as we entered Leeds—by invitation. Just as in 1819 W. Clowes found his way to Leeds because Messrs. Verity, S. Smith and others had sent a letter addressed to " the Ranter Preacher, Hull," asking that they might be supplied with a preacher, so in 1825 W. Clowes entered Cornwall as the first Primitive Methodist missionary in response to a request. It came from Mr. Turner who, like the Leeds band of young men, had been working on Primitive Methodist lines though unattached to any religious community. That was how we entered the " delectable Duchy."

Tunstall Circuit Resumes Missionary Operations.— In 1819 Tunstall Circuit freed itself from the fetters of the Non-Mission Law and took up aggressive work with great vigour. It was time ; for at the close of 1818 the membership was only 490 more than it had been seven years before. A notable Camp Meeting at Wrine Hill on the Cheshire border ushered in the Great Revival which did so much for the enlargement of the Connexion. Fitting instruments were ready to carry on the work as well as to conserve its gains. John Wedgewood was now a veteran in revival experience and had returned to Staffordshire full of ardour. Also there were Hugh Bourne's " boys," as half affectionately and half contemptuously some called them ; such as John Garner, Thomas Jackson (1), Sampson Turner, and James Bonser. And then, too, there was Hugh Bourne himself, now recovered from his illness and depression, ready to toil, and eager to put the ideas with which his brain was teeming into shape. A general advance was made. The Circuit all round its wide circumference pushed back its frontiers until it became unwieldy, and in fifteen months it was found needful to divide it into five branches. Better than material enlargement was the encouraging increase of 1,013 members for the fifteen months. What, however, concerns us now is, to note the extent to which the Revival contributed

to the permanent enlargement of the Connexion
First of all, from Cannock as the base, a sure footing
was at once gained in the Black Country by the
formation in 1820 of the Darlaston Circuit.   It was
founded in persecution—magisterial as distinct from
popular—and perhaps it was founded all the more
solidly for that reason.   Darlaston became one of
the powerful, procreant Circuits of the Connexion,
and one of the widest, operating as it did over a
tract of country extending from Birmingham and
Worcester as far as to Presteign in Radnorshire.
The district about and north of Delamere Forest
was vigorously missioned, and in 1823 Preston
Brook Circuit was formed, which in turn lent a
hand to the missioning of Liverpool, also sending,
in 1832, F. N. Jersey to Ireland.   The CHESHIRE
MISSION, as by eminence it was called, was begun
in the spring of 1819 by John Wedgewood.   The
countryside was moved at his coming.   His open-
air, and even his early morning, services drew
crowds ; many fell to the ground under the power
of the Word.   Abstemious, tireless, restless, he did
not tarry long at one place, but moved northwards,
leaving to others the gathering of the converts into
Societies.   "In its grand results," says Thomas
Bateman, writing of the Cheshire Mission, "it has
but seldom been exceeded."   From this time began
Thomas Bateman's own attachment and unique
service to the Connexion which was to last almost
as long as the century.   Burland from 1823 became
the mother of Circuits.   From it sprang Liverpool,
where John Ride was imprisoned, and Chester

(1825) ; while by its Shropshire Mission it laid the foundation for the many Circuits which have developed from the old Prees Green Circuit.

We now turn to another side of the Tunstall Circuit. The early, occasional visits of Eleazar Hathorn to Manchester were soon followed by a determined effort to gain a permanent footing in the big town. In 1820, through the pioneer labours of the Brownswords (brother and sister), Bonser, Verity and Carter, the town and neighbourhood were energetically missioned. Despite the long and serious imprisonment of Mr. S. Waller, the people gladly heard the Gospel message. Manchester was made a Circuit and by 1842 had multiplied to eight, namely Manchester, Bolton with its offshoot the Isle of Man, Oldham, Stockport, Bury, Rochdale and Staleybridge. Tunstall's mission to the coal and iron districts of South Shropshire resulted in the making, in 1823, of Oakengates Circuit. From Oakengates, 1823, sprang the distant mission to Blaenavon in South Wales, which in its turn planted our Church at Cwm—ever memorable as the scene of the devoted labours of Thomas Proctor—Hereford and the Forest of Dean. From Shrewsbury, made from Oakengates in 1824, came not only Bishop's Castle and other Shropshire stations, but also the establishment of the Wiltshire Mission by S. Heath (1824), the making of the famous Brinkworth Circuit and all that came of it. Last, it is to be noted that, in 1823, Tunstall joined with Scotter in establishing the Western Mission which from Stroud in Gloucestershire branched out to Bath, Frome in

Somerset, Motcombe in Dorset, and Salisbury in South Wilts. We are now in Thomas Hardy's country, and at Poole are within sight of the English Channel. Under John Ride's fine leadership the movement is eastwards. London is evidently the objective. If it were not strategy it looks very much like it. In 1833 Brinkworth is made a District with fifteen Circuits in ten different counties.

Nottingham Circuit and its Missionary Extensions. —The Factory at Broad Marsh (superseded by old Canaan Street 1823) became the centre of a strong and aggressive society having at its head a staff of capable officials. As early as 1818 Gainsborough and those parts of north Lincolnshire that lie west of the old Roman highway of Ermine Street were well missioned by William Braithwaite and Thomas Saxton, while the next year Thomas King and others laid the foundations of the Market Rasen, Grimsby, Louth and Alford Circuits. Loughborough as a gain of the Revival of 1817–18 became a base for the evangelisation of the regions beyond. The plan of 1822 has on it forty-two places out of which some dozen Circuits have been formed. Northward, Jeremiah Gilbert was sent to Sheffield and Hallamshire. Other labourers were thrust into the field and, by 1824, a wide district had been missioned, namely Sheffield, Barnsley, Chesterfield, Wakefield, Halifax, Bradwell, Doncaster and Huddersfield. South-east Lincolnshire also fell to Nottingham.

In 1821 Messrs. Oscroft and Charlton, deeming the Lincolnshire branches overmanned, skirted the

Wash and began missioning in NORFOLK. By 1823 Nottingham had six branches in this direction—Boston, Spalding, Norwich, Fakenham, Cambridge and Lynn. Of these, with Yarmouth and Upwell added, Norwich District was constituted in 1825 with thirteen ministers. By 1833, under the labours of such men as John Smith (1), Thomas Batty and Robert Key, it had thirteen stations, thirty-six missionaries and 5,948 members. So by the time of Queen Victoria's accession it had fairly covered East Anglia, reached into Essex and Hunts., and from 1828 to 1834, London with its Kent missions stood on its District stations ; and we note that John Oscroft, one of the pioneers of the Norwich District, was the superintendent of London Circuit from 1830 to 1834.

Methods of Circuit Propagation—" Branches " and " Circuit Missions."—The geographical extension of the early years proceeded by a twofold method, of which we may perhaps find the analogues in organic chemistry. In the yeast-cell we see a process of multiplication by budding going on. Each cell gives out one or two little germinations from its side. These grow larger by degrees and receive into themselves part of the contents of the parent-cell. Then these split off, but not before they themselves have given rise to buds, and these in their turn to others, so that you have branching chains of linked cells. Then, too, we are familiar with multiplication by offshoots or by dissemination, as when the thistledown is wafted to a favouring spot and so finds its nidus, or a shoot springs from the parent-root in an unexpected quarter. The " Branch " system, which so largely obtained after 1819, was a form of multiplication by budding. The " Home Branch," as it was called, exercised rights of jurisdiction over the most distant Branch, while, for local purposes, that Branch had independence and the right of initiative. By this system competent advisers were available for an emergency. Interchanges between the Branches could easily be effected, and the monetary deficiencies made up. In " Circuit Missions " we have multiplication by offshoots or seedlings. This second method of propagation, contributed to geographical extension in a rapid and effective way. Hull had its missions in Kent and on both sides of the Solent, in Bedford and Herts., in Cornwall, and twice over in London. For years it issued an annual Report like a miniature Missionary Society. Sunderland missioned Edinburgh (1823), Carlisle missioned Glasgow (1826), Newcastle—Dundee (1836), Bolton—The Isle of Man (1823), and Burland —Northampton. Nor must we forget the boldest venture of all when, in 1829, Hull and Tunstall Circuits combined in sending four missionaries to the United States. Their equipment included a supply of hand-bills which were to make known to the inhabitants of America the fact and purport of their coming !

Sometimes the missionary was left with a free hand. So in 1824 Leicester set apart two missionaries to mission—somewhere ! They were " to follow

the directions of Divine Providence." After re-
connoitring the country they set up their standard
at Witney, the blanket-town.   In the same uncal-
culating way Saffron Walden was reached by
Downham Circuit's missionaries.

We have now, perhaps, said enough to convey to
the reader a general idea of three things, namely—
How far Primitive Methodism had succeeded in
establishing itself in the year 1833 when Brinkworth
District was formed ; by what lines of direction
it got thus far ; and what were the methods of
propaganda, commended and tested by experience,
which had enabled it to extend itself thus far.   A
still more important inquiry now awaits us.

E

CHAPTER V.

The Spirit of the Pioneers and their Probation of Toil and Suffering.

> " It takes a soul
> To move a body : it takes a high-souled man
> To move the masses . . . even to a cleaner stye :
> It takes the ideal, to blow a hair's-breadth off
> The dust of the actual.—Ah, your Fouriers failed
> Because not poets enough to understand
> That life develops from within."
>
> ELIZABETH BARRETT BROWNING.

I.   OUR FATHERS' SECRET SOURCE OF POWER.

What Manner of Men were the Pioneers ?—By what means was it brought about that by Queen Victoria's accession Primitive Methodism had covered, or earmarked, so much of English ground ? It is not enough to say " The Circuits did it." We must beware of loose thinking lest we end with imperfect realisation. The real dynamic of energy was not an abstraction called a " Circuit " ; it was in the souls of a band of men who responded to the same evangelic impulse which prompted Hugh Bourne's Christmas Sermon. They, like him, had the genuine " missionary rudiment "—the unquenchable desire to " seek the wandering souls of men." As the desire grew it became an energy and moved them to go farther afield to give it play and scope. Their methods of propaganda were simple in the extreme, yet they were handy, flexible, and they served their purpose. They had absorbed some of the ruling ideas of the founders and did their best to apply them. We know some of the watchwords of the time : " Seek to bring a variety of talents into lively exercise ' ; " No sex in Church work " ; " Look well after the children " ; " Be prepared for spiritual conflicts, and learn how to take upon you the burthen of souls " ; " Exercise faith in silence " ; " Practise Conversation-Preaching diligently, at home and abroad ; but don't bungle the work or suffer it to become a form." When they stood up publicly, on camp-ground, in barn or cottage, at village-cross or in the street, they proclaimed " a full, free and present salvation " ; they looked for results. They were schooled to rely on no adventitious aids such as flags or drums and trumpets, and the lesson seems to have been very thoroughly learned ; for, all down the years, resort to such material means for drawing attention and impressing the people seems to have been discouraged, while the occasional offenders were brought under discipline and solemnly admonished.* But, though the pioneer preachers carried no flag and blew no trumpet, they never failed to carry with them their hymn-book as well as Bible, and as a rule they needed no one to raise the tune, but were their own precentors. Many of them could say with William Clowes, " My soul's full of music," and they got it well out of them. The old hymns did no little to banish

* As at Grimsby. See Clowes' " Journal," p. 316.

the lewd and immoral song, and were a most important factor in sweetening life and in spreading and commending the Gospel. How many like C. C. M'Kechnie were " sung into the Kingdom " in those early days !

Intercessory Prayer : Braithwaite and Oxtoby.— To leave out this factor would be unpardonable. Though the missionary might seem a very harmless kind of man and ill-qualified whether for defence or offence, he was invisibly armed with the weapon of all-prayer.   There were many things the pioneers could not do ; but they did know how to wrestle and prevail ; and there is a close connection between that statement and the map of Primitive Methodism as it was in 1832–33.   We are reminded, as we write these words, of what followed William Braithwaite's overheard prayer from behind the hedge at East Stockwith : " Thou must give me souls ; I cannot preach without souls ; Lord, give me souls or I shall die."   We think, too, of John Oxtoby's sublimely audacious prayer which heralded the wonderful moral transformation of Filey and its fishermen. As we have written elsewhere, Muston Hill was Oxtoby's Peniel, only—and in this he was nobler than Jacob—he wrestled on behalf of others, and not for himself.   We would not suggest that sweeping revivals of religion were confined to the first period of our Connexional history.   That is not the case ; God be thanked !   But whenever and wherever genuine revivals have occurred, we may be sure that intercessory prayer has been at the heart of them. To this the experience of such men of prayer of a later date as Atkinson Smith, William Lonsdale, Parkinson Milson and George Warner sufficiently testify. This said, we turn to what must ever be regarded as the classic examples in our annals of intercessory prayer fronting an apparently hopeless prospect, yet bearing up and in the end wringing victory from threatening defeat. We revert, then, to Wessex and East Anglia in the days (1830–33) when the rick-burners and machine-breakers were at their fell work. It was in 1838 that Cobden wrote : " The great body of the English peasantry are not yet a whit advanced in intellect since the days of their Saxon ancestors." Indeed ! If this allegation were true, whose was the blame ? But, in truth, the indictment was a little belated ; for by that time both in Wessex and East Anglia the leaven had been put in and was already working to such results that Professor Thorold Rogers and Dr. Dykes and Canon Jessop could ungrudgingly testify that, to Primitive Methodism was mainly due the rescue from semi-heathenism and the moral and intellectual quickening of the peasantry of Southern and Eastern England. The results of the Revival of the 'thirties in these parts will bear comparison with those of the Midland and Northern Revivals of 1817–24—great though those results were in the judgment of competent and unbiassed witnesses.

The Ashdown Pleading : " Lord, Give us Berkshire ! "—We take a leap of seven years, and from

Muston Hill, overlooking Filey Bay, we transport ourselves to Ashdown on the Berkshire Downs. The time and the place are alike significant. For the place, it was associated with memories of Alfred and his victory over the Danes gained nearly a thousand years before. For the time, it was the February of 1830—that stormy year, when disaffection and the antagonism of classes seemed to have reached their height. A few months hence, in the once royal city of Winchester lying over yonder, three hundred wretched men will be tried at a special assize, with the Duke of Wellington present to support the judges. Of these poor peasants, six were actually sentenced to suffer on the gallows ; twenty were transported for life, the remainder for periods varying according to judicial discretion. *The Times* of December 27th, 1830—all praise to it—spoke out in solemn protest :—" The present population must be provided for in body and spirit on more liberal and Christian principles, or the whole mass of labourers will start into legions of a banditti —banditti less criminal than those who have made them so—than those who by a just and fearful retribution will soon become their victims." It was on the very threshold of such happenings as these that Brinkworth Circuit resolved on a forward movement ; to attempt the very work which, according to *The Times*, so urgently needed doing in these southern counties, if insurrection was to be avoided. The situation was one of immense difficulty. The missionaries were likely to be misjudged by both sides, and to find themselves between two fires, as indeed happened. On a dull, cheerless day, then, in November, 1830, John Ride, the superintendent of Brinkworth, and Thomas Russell, his young colleague, are to be seen approaching Ashdown Park Corner, where the treeless, rolling downs are varied by a coppice or small wood. The younger man already that morning had walked ten miles across the downs to meet his companion for prayer and counsel, and they were now returning together. Reaching the wood, they had to part, as their destinations lay in different directions. They had already shaken hands. But no ; they must not—should not—part, until it had been fought out on their knees whether their mission was to prosper. " Let us turn in here and have another round of prayer before we part," was the proposal of one of them, and turning aside into the coppice, and screened by the underwood and far from any habitation, no more secluded spot for communion with God could be found. Unmindful of the snow and of personal considerations, they throw themselves on their knees, and in an agony pour out their souls to God. The success of their mission, which is for God's honour and the salvation of souls, is summed up in the burden of their prayer : " Lord, give us Berkshire ! Lord, give us Berkshire." The pleading continued for hours. At last the younger one receives the assurance and, rising to his feet, exclaims with an outburst that betokens a new-found possession : " Yonder country's ours ! Yonder country's ours ! and we will have it," as he points across the country bounded by the Hamp-

shire hills some thirty miles distant. " Hold fast !
I like thy confidence of faith," is the response of
the more sober pleader. They now part with the
assurance that " yonder country *is* ours."

The sequel to this spiritual struggle was similar
to that of Oxtoby's pleading for Filey. The next
day Thomas Russell found himself at Shefford,
where God opened the heart of Mr. and Mrs. Wells.
They built a house which became a home for the
preachers and also served as a place of worship.
In 1832 Shefford became a Circuit, with John Ride
as its superintendent. It was made a new base
for missionary extension, and in 1835 it had no
fewer than eighteen preachers labouring under
the direction of its quarterly meeting. From a
strategical point of view our history can show
nothing finer than the long-sustained movement
by which from Brinkworth *via* Shefford and Reading,
with side-movements into Hampshire and Oxford-
shire, Primitive Methodism by dint of hard labour
and through much persecution made its way through
the home counties and on to the very environs
of London. Of that movement, extending over
nineteen years, John Ride was the chief director.
May we not say that the spiritual wrestle at Ashdown was at the root of this remarkable movement ?
Once more :

Robert Key's Remarkable Conflict of Soul while
preaching at Saham Toney in 1832 throws us back
for an explanation on the views of Crawfoot and
Hugh Bourne as to the nature of spiritual conflicts.

The heavy oppressive cloud which seemed to enwrap Key while he spoke, dulling all feeling and stifling all his powers except faith in God—that cloud broke at last, and under the manifest power of God sinners were forced either to yield or rush from the room. On that night a distinct link was forged in the providential chain of events which led up to the conversion of C. H. Spurgeon in 1850. One of the night's converts was a young woman whose changed exemplary life led her brother to Christ. That brother was Robert Eaglen, who in Colchester Primitive Methodist Chapel was the honoured instrument in pointing Spurgeon to the Lamb of God. Our fathers believed, and acted under the belief, that to them it was given, by means of prayer and faith, to wield the mightiest of spiritual forces.

II. THE PROBATIONARY PERIOD OF TOIL, PRIVATION AND PERSECUTION.

" None of us knows what truth is until we suffer for it; neither do we know what we ourselves are and what Allies we have beyond space and time."

JOHN A. HUTTON, M.A.

We can bring to thought the England of our denominational pioneers only by a strong effort. How many things we have to leave out of the picture we now reckon as indispensable! We have to eliminate the useful lucifer-match, gas as an illuminant of our homes and streets, the ramifications of our railway system, our ocean steamers, the electric telegraph and the penny post. All

these and more were to make their appearance
together towards the end of our period and the
beginning of Victoria's long reign. They were to
transform the face of the country, facilitate inter-
course, and make the conditions of life brighter and
easier. But our fathers began their mission before
the era of flint and steel and the horn lantern had
passed. There was, to be sure, the stage-coach
running on the main roads, but this mode of con-
veyance did not suit the pocket, or, usually, the
convenience of the missionary who wanted to carry
the Gospel along the byways and among the
sequestered villages which the coach left aside.
So it was inevitable that Primitive Methodism
should be spread by a pedestrianising propaganda,
on a scale such as had not been known since
Wycliffe's " poor preachers " had itinerated the
country. It is not hard to conceive what all this
involved, in all weathers, year in and year out, in
the way of exposure, discomfort and fatigue.

" *In Hunger and Thirst, in Fastings often.*"—Toil
and discomfort, we may be sure, were cheerfully
borne, as inseparable from the missionary's lot ;
the more so, as he often shared the discomfort with
those to whom he ministered. It was another
thing when to mere fatigue and discomfort was
added positive hunger. As a genuine document,
touching in its simplicity, nothing can beat the
account Joseph Reynolds sent to the Tunstall
Circuit of how he had fared and felt while missioning
in and around Cambridge. The letter, which might

have been written by a suffering follower of George Fox long ago, deserves a paragraph to itself. The date is August, 1821 :—

" Dear Brethren,—When I left Tunstall, I gave myself up to labour and sufferings, and I have gone through both ; but, praise the Lord, it has been for His glory and the good of souls. My sufferings are known only to God and myself. I have many times been knocked down while preaching, and have often had sore bones. Once I was knocked down and was trampled under the feet of the crowd, and had my clothes torn and all my money taken from me. In consequence of this I have been obliged to suffer much hunger. One day I travelled nearly thirty miles and had only a penny cake to eat. I preached at night to nearly two thousand persons. But I was so weak when I had done, that I could scarcely stand. I then made my supper of cold cabbage, and slept under a haystack in a field till about four o'clock in the morning. The singing of the birds then awoke me, and I arose and went into the town, and preached at five to many people. I afterwards came to Cambridge, where I have been a fortnight, and preached to a great congregation, though almost worn out with fatigue and hunger. To-day I was glad to eat the pea-husks as I walked on the road. But I bless God that much good has been done. I believe that hundreds will have to bless Him in eternity for leading me hither."

" *With Persecutions.*"—But the worst evils endured by our early missionaries may be summed up in the word *Persecution,* which was rife throughout this period. They suffered from the petty annoyances of the mischievous, who deemed them fair game ; from the brutality of the mob ; from priestly intolerance ; from the straining and maladministration of the law. The hymn raised by the missionary and his few supporters was often the signal for interruptions by " fellows of the baser sort," and even for the interference of some who would have resented being classed as such. To make a noise—the bigger the better—was felt to be the only right thing to do. So, the bells were set a-ringing to drown the preacher's voice ; sometimes so vigorously that the bells cracked. Tins and kettles were banged and clashed, or drums beaten. At Witney Camp Meeting forty horns were being blown at once. At Dalton-in-Furness, while F N Jersey was praying at the Cross, three horns and a watchman's rattle made such a din in the preacher's ears as to cause him to shout on rising from his knees, " Glory be to Jesus ! I can praise Thee amidst all the din of hell." At ducal Bottesford a dog-fight was got up, and at Sandbach a bull was headed for the congregation in the field ; but it would persist in kneeling down some distance off as if to do obeisance.

When we come to missile-throwing we leave rowdyism for ruffianism—the attempt at disturbance for PERSONAL MALTREATMENT. " Rage has weapons always nigh." Stones are plentiful and handy. At Lincoln, William Clowes was made to bleed with one. At Market Rasen shot was slung. But rotten eggs were the favourite missiles, as at Oxford, where Mr. Bellham and his colleagues were so besmeared that they had to go to the pump to cleanse themselves with a wisp of straw. Perhaps the two worst cases of brutal handling by the mob on record in our annals are those in which John Garner and Thomas Russell were the victims. The former case occurred at Sowe, near Coventry, in 1819, at the very outset of Mr. Garner's ministry. It was a veritable man-baiting, and the poor youth—he was only nineteen—was left half dead. He was ultimately rescued and nursed to convalescence by kindly cottagers. When able to move about again he noticed that his thrifty persecutors had made his tattered garments do duty in their gardens as scare-crows ! The second case is even worse than the first—if that be possible. Thomas Russell was hunted and roughly handled by the mob at Wantage and Shrivenham in April 1830. So prolonged and savage was his treatment that he almost despaired of coming out of it alive. With this reference to incidents well-nigh too revolting for recital we pass on.

Attempts at Indirect Repression.—We have now to glance at suffering of a different kind—less revolting indeed to outward appearance, but more subtle in its working, involving greater suffering, and from its very nature harder to deal with. We refer to the persecution which sought to get at the missionary through his helpers and sympathisers. Clericalism and landlordism, or both acting in concert, often unmercifully applied the screw. Local preachers received notice to quit their holdings ; those who opened their cottages for preaching were evicted ; to show hospitality to the preacher—above all to give him a night's shelter—was to run the risk of becoming homeless or workless. To spare his people, the preacher in the pioneer days of the Berkshire Mission had often to walk many a weary mile in order to secure a night's shelter out of reach

of the squire or parson's boycott.   Here is a picture
of clerical intolerance and rural subservience in the
Hampshire of the 'thirties—and what a picture it is !
Undeterred by the parson's threat of prosecution
should he dare to preach in his parish, Mr. Watts
set out for the village.   The clerical autocrat went
round to his parishioners ordering them to keep
indoors and have every door and window shut.
And they did as they were told; so that as the
missionary passed along he might have thought
the village had been swept by plague, so sad and
silent did it seem.   As late as 1878 John Bright
affirmed that there were more than two thousand
places in England where Dissenters could not get
a plot of ground to build a chapel on because the
parson and the squire worked together, " and,"
he remarked, " they are Siamese Twins."   In the
'thirties the Twins were bolder than they are now,
in the Southern counties at any rate.

" *In Prisons more Frequent.*"—Only one thing
more is wanting to complete the picture—there
must be a prison in the background ; and it is forth-
coming.   In Mr. Petty's " History," within the
period ending 1843 there are distinct references to
thirty cases of arrest for open-air preaching, ending,
sometimes in detention, and occasionally in imprisonment with hard labour.   These thirty cases
are not all that might be adduced by any means.
Most of the early preachers had one such experience.
To some of them the interference of the constable
became quite a familiar incident ; so familiar as to

excite neither surprise nor alarm. The first Sunday
Jeremiah Gilbert began his labours—May 1819—
he was "taken up" at Bolsover, in Derbyshire,
along with Samuel Atterby, and lodged in prison.
Two years later we find him saying : " In the last
fifteen months I have been taken before the magis-
trates for preaching the Gospel six or seven times,
but I have never lost anything but pride, shame,
unbelief, hardness of heart, the fear of man, love of
the world, and prejudice of mind. I have always
come out of prison more pure than when I went in."
In their relations with the magistracy and police,
the missionaries showed to great advantage. They
had developed readiness of resource and the acuteness
of lawyers. Moreover, they knew they were on the
right side and that they were fighting the battle
of religious liberty. This conviction gave them
calmness and confidence in the presence of those
who sought to abridge their liberties. Nor can we
forbear believing that when apprehended they
rather enjoyed the ill-disguised perplexity of the
Justice Shallows of the period to know what to
do with their prisoner. They secretly chuckled
as they saw the magistrate, helped by his clerk,
referring to musty precedents, fumbling with law-
books, and getting mixed with statutes of Elizabeth
and Charles II.

" *Prison-Scenes from the Lives of our Early
Missionaries* " would make a fitting companion-
volume to " Camp Meeting Idylls." Somehow we
find there is brightness and cheerfulness and melody

in the prison.   We feel the man in the prison needs
our pity less than the men who put him in.   When
the missionary was interrupted in his open-air
preaching his invariable practice was to avoid all
insolence; firmly, but respectfully, to stand on his
rights and refuse to compromise.   When led off
to prison he sang all the way there, and beguiled
the tedium of confinement by still more singing.
Then, when liberated, he usually made his way
straight to the place at which he had been pulled
down, and held another service.   This was what
Jeremiah Gilbert did when arrested at Eckington
in Derbyshire on July 12th, 1820.   He was thrust
into a damp and doleful room.   The door was
studded with nails, and a barred aperture served
for a window.   When he was not exhorting the
people gathered outside, he was singing with them.
Later on he conversed with the jailer about the
salvation of his soul and prayed with him.   About
midnight he blocked up the makeshift of a window
as well as he could, and, failing better accommodation, he lay on some laths with a besom for his
pillow.   After his release he stood up to preach
near the place where he had been pulled down,
and had a large and attentive congregation.

A Possible Map of the Persecution Area.—If a
map were drawn and tinted to show the comparative
amount of persecution our denomination has met
with in the different parts of England, the most
northerly counties would show to greatest advantage.
Thus, while on some parts of the map there might

be found only streaks and patches of colour, some of the southern counties would be washed with the distinguishing tint. It would also be found that persecution was the most bitter, general and inveterate in precisely those districts where dissent had the least hold and influence, and where the cleavage between the upper and lower classes was most complete. Once more it would be found that where the Church, as by law established, had for long had its own way, unchecked and unthwarted by " schism," there the people were little better than serfs, and there persecution was rampant. Note the reception Messrs. Clough and Lister met with at Berwick-on-Tweed in 1829, when they preached to thousands of people, including the clergy and gentry of the town ; contrast their treatment with that meted out to our missionaries in Hants, Wilts., Berks., and other southern counties. In Northumberland there was too much Presbyterianism, in the eastern counties there was too much Puritanism, and in Cornwall there was too much Methodism for persecution to be anything else but short-lived, though these, too, were non-manufacturing districts. The Rev. Thomas Binney discharged an explosive shell into the religious world when, in 1833, he declared that the " principle " of the national religious establishment " destroys more souls than it saves ; and therefore its end is to be devoutly wished by every lover of God and man." We do not know whether Mr. Binney was aware of what was going on not very far from him when he penned these words. If he were, there was some

F

excuse for them. In the sense intended, the words amount almost to a truism ; and it is the simple truth to say that the early history of our Church is a heavy indictment of the State Church. In our annals of persecution, the clergyman comes on the scene with almost sickening frequency. But yet charity would put in a demurrer. Every clergyman was not a persecutor in grain. It was a clergyman who, when he gave Sampson Turner his license to preach the Gospel, said, "Mind you preach it plainly." It was another clergyman who said when the missionary had entered his village, " My curate has come." True, but as one swallow does not make a summer, so the few exceptional clergymen and squires and constables we read of as countenancing and sympathising with the Primitive Methodist missionary serve only, like points of light, to make the surrounding darkness yet more pitchy dark.

As we end this section, who can wonder that in many cases the missionary, like Thomas Proctor, died early, or that the strongest, like John Garner, never threw off the effects of the inhuman treatment to which they had been subjected ?

III. THE CRISIS OF 1825–8 : ITS CAUSES AND ITS LESSONS.

" The winds blow and beat against the house ; yet it does not fall."

MATT. VII. 25 (Weymouth's Version).

Trouble from Within as well as from Without.— " Beside those things that are without, there is that which presseth upon me daily, anxiety for all the churches." So wrote Paul to the Corinthians, and the leaders of our Church were in much the same situation as this in 1825–8. It does seem strange that, in a period of such extraordinary enlargement and triumph over all kinds of adverse conditions, trouble should start up from within. But so it was. Until this crisis was got through and left behind, Primitive Methodism's Probation was not ended or its " expectation of life " complete. That there was such a crisis is no mere fancy ; the evidence is abundant and conclusive. Even before the echoes of the Revivals of 1817–24 had died away, the crisis began to show itself ; and probably it was in the Midlands where the signs of what was coming became recognisable. For three years in succession no returns of membership were given—an ominous sign. That the preparation of the Deed Poll was so long delayed must be accounted for in the same way. What was the good of a Deed of Settlement when the Connexion itself was in such an unsettled state ? The manuscript Journals of both Hugh Bourne and Thomas Bateman reveal the gravity of the situation and the searchings of heart it occasioned. Anxious consultations between the elder and younger man took place. Fears were interchanged as to the stability and permanence of the Connexion. " No one for a time could tell how to keep it up for another twelve months," wrote Hugh Bourne, who was well-nigh heart-broken at the outlook. Jonathan Ireland, too, gives confirmatory evidence. He tells us that from 1825 to 1828 " the Connexion was in a tottering state, and many who watched its move-

ments and knew its internal condition were really
of opinion that it would collapse and fall." So,
fearing for " the soundness of the Connexion, my
friend and I endeavoured to dissuade George Lamb
of Preston, a local preacher of some eminence, from
entering the ministry as he desired."* As to its
causes, the Crisis was brought about by defective
discipline and financial recklessness or slackness :
it was largely an economic crisis. Men had crept
into the societies, some of them the mischief-makers
of other Churches, who lusted after the exercise
of power. The demand for preachers had been
abnormal; but now the ministry needed purging
of its drones and ineffectives. By 1826 the
mischief had reached its height. At the Conference
of that year drastic emergency measures were
taken. In twelve months no less than thirty
preachers were parted with. " Runners-out of
Circuits " was Hugh Bourne's expressive phrase
for them. By 1827 the worst was over : the " drag
was taken off the wheels," and the chariot rolled
on again, as the increases for 1832 and 1833 testify—
namely, 4,185 and 7,120. 1832 was quite as notable
a year as 1819 in many regards. But we fasten on
one feature of its Bradford Conference: Now the
Deed Poll members first took their seats, and it was
ordered that the Deed Poll itself should be printed
" in octavo, at five shillings a copy, in extra boards."
Small things these, it may be said. Small in them-

---

* But George Lamb did not yield to their dissuasives. See
" Jonathan Ireland the Street Preacher : an Autobiography,"
pp. 50 and 82.

selves—yes ; but not small in what they signified. They were signs and seals of restored confidence ; vouchers that the Connexion had at last, through the toils and persecutions and inner conflicts of a score of years, gained the consciousness that its work was by no means done, and that God was going to give it a future. That was a great assurance —a thing to be thankful for. On these notes of assurance and thankfulness the Period of Probation ends.

CHAPTER VI.

A Yeasty, Transition Period—1832-60.

> " As to the weather of 1832, the Zadkiels of that time had predicted that the electrical condition of the clouds in the political hemisphere would produce unusual perturbations in organic existence, and he would perhaps have seen a fulfilment of his remarkable prophecy in the mutual influence of dissimilar destinies which we shall see gradually unfolding itself."
>
> GEORGE ELIOT, *Felix Holt.*

I. THE "TIME-SPIRIT" OF THE THIRTIES.

Primitive Methodism's "Sturm und Drang" Period. —The score and odd years that followed 1832 do not readily lend themselves to classification. They do not seem to fit nicely into any scheme of periods. They are intractable and something of a puzzle. To call them " The Middle Years " would not help us much; since to a Church which is living, and likely to live, the middle years of its history can have no fixity, but must ever be moving on as the Church grows older. We are inclined to believe that the key to the puzzle may be found in the peculiar " time-spirit " prevailing in the 'thirties of last century. The time-spirit is a very subtile and penetrative thing, and not even a Church can escape its influence. On the contrary, it is almost as sensitive to what is going on around it as is the barometer to atmospheric pressure. This said—to our clue. In his " Life of Richard Cobden," Lord Morley dwells on the remarkable character of the ten years which followed the passing of the Reform Bill. That eagerly-expected measure did not fulfil expectations. Instead of the Millennium it ushered in a time of disillusionment. Yet the experience seemed to be tonic rather than lowering. It led to a marvellous increase of activity in numberless fields of thought and endeavour. Lord Morley even goes so far as to say : " The result of the disappointment was such a degree of activity among all the better minds of the time that the succeeding generation, say from 1840 to 1870, practically lived upon the thought and the sentiment of the seven or eight years immediately preceding the close of the Liberal reign in 1841. . . . *It was now the day of ideals in every camp."* He proceeds to make good his suggestive generalisation by giving an array of names—of men and books, of diverse schools of thought and movements. We forbear quotation and cannot stay to summarise ; but will just remind ourselves that the abortive Chartist movement, the Oxford movement which has wrought so much both of good and ill, the founding of the Free Church of Scotland, and, a little later, the troubles and disruptions of the mother-Church of Methodism— all fall within this period. The fact is, a new England was coming to birth, and the Old and New were often in conflict. It was not to be expected that Primitive Methodism would escape the contagion of the times ; nor did it. It was for it a period of perturbation and, because it was that, it was also a period of transition. The key seems to fit, and it is of psychological make.

Some " Splits " of the Period.—It was in the year 1851, the Great Exhibition year, that Charles Kingsley published his " Yeast." Both the title and contents of this brilliant novel are descriptive of the strange fermentation that was going on in the body politic at the time. It was, too, a yeasty period in Primitive Methodism. It had its heady spirits who protested up to breaking-point and were prepared to follow their ideals, such as they were, regardless of consequences. Hence, Primitive Methodism has had its " splitlets " (" splits " is too big, a word for them) and many of them fall within this period. The disastrous schism on the Edinburgh Mission had occurred as early as 1828, and the Independent Primitive Methodists set up for themselves at Bingham and the surrounding villages about the same time. We note these " splitlets " here for convenience. But falling properly within this period, we have the Denmanite secession at Leicester which carried off sixty-five members (1833–6). There were troubles at Nottingham in 1834 in which the junior minister William Antliff won his spurs, and swiftly rose to be a leading figure in the Connexion all through this and the following period. In 1838, in Belper Circuit, the Selstonites broke off on a question of salary—should it be raised from sixteen to eighteen shillings per week ? Then we have the pamphlet-war and troubles, both in Hull and Leeds, which followed the expulsion of the zealous but unmanageable John Stamp in 1841. The only splitlet we know of that turned on a purely doctrinal question—and that a minor one—occurred at Oswestry in 1846. Then, too, we have to chronicle the secession at Scotter in 1849 which lost to us the historic chapel where "the good" Conference of 1829 held its sittings. Finally, the oddest splitlet of all was "The Old Hymn-Bookers" who would not have the Hymn Book of 1853 at any price, and broke off to form societies at St. Mary Bourne and other villages in the Andover Circuit in Hampshire.

Discussions and Controversies on Organisation and Administration that might ruffle the calm of the Connexion but did not imperil its unity were common in this restless, seminal period. Of these the two that call for special mention both pivoted on what we may call the Exclusiveness and Seclusiveness of the Conference. Only hearers who possessed certain high qualifications in their own Circuits, and who also carried passports that were carefully scanned by the doorkeepers, could gain admission. Then as to delegateship : only superintendents of comparatively long standing, and the higher grades of officials who had been such for a given length of time, were eligible for election. The Conference was thus an assembly of elders both as to age and status ; and this was not always an advantage when so much new wine was being vinted and wanted bottling. Able, but younger men, found themselves ineligible for their own highest court and had to wait almost until grey hairs for the right of entry. C. C. M'Kechnie did not get to Conference at all within this period, although he began his ministry in

1838. By the stringent law of 1845 only those preachers who had travelled eighteen years, and been superintendents for twelve, were pronounced as qualified for election ; and it was not until 1865 that this strait law was relaxed. Conference did not lay itself out to be popular in those days. The crowd was permitted to gather at the Camp ground and flock to the public meetings, but the Conference hedged itself about with restrictions. This policy was sure to be attended by its appropriate Nemesis. District Meetings stood to gain in popularity at the expense of Conferences, just as they also stood to gain by the division and multiplication of Circuits. In this same year 1845, an Association was formed to modify the state of things by enrolling members, sending up petitions, and by repeated legislation (which was as repeatedly thrown out). The Association proposed that preachers of fifteen years' standing who had been superintendents ten successive years should have voice and vote at Conference on condition they paid their own expenses. John Bywater was the Secretary of the Association and John Flesher was one of its members. The minutes of the Association are in the writer's possession. Relief, however, was not to come by way of the Association's proposals but by the liberalising and enlarging of Conference by its own act and deed. The Hymn Book Controversy of 1853–4 was threatening while it lasted, but by some concessions— including some cancelling and some verbal changes— on the part of the London authorities it was in the end amicably settled. The non-contents in this case were leading men in the North, both ministers and laymen, and the gravamen of their complaint was that the Hymn Book had been sprung upon the Connexion and was not worthy of it. As to the latter charge it is piquant to find the " intellectuals " of the Sunderland district and the Old Hymn-Bookers of Hampshire in hearty agreement. Here we leave the controversy, which is more fully described in the larger " History " of our Church. It is only just to add that, whatever blemishes it may have had, the Hymn Book of 1853 aided the worship of our Church for a generation.

II. EXTENSION BEYOND THE SEAS

" This English Exodus has been the greatest English event of the eighteenth and nineteenth centuries."

PROFESSOR J. R. SEELEY.

Following the Tide of Emigration.—In the 'forties of last century the tide of emigration began to flow with ever-increasing volume. From 1853 to 1888, 1,324,018 emigrants left British ports for Australasia, and 912,477 for British North America. Many of our adherents were counted in these vast totals. The religion of some of these might have been labelled " perishable," for it did not survive the long voyage. But the religion of others was of a hardier type and remained unaffected by the break-up of old associations and the novel scenes they found themselves amongst. They kept the old

fire burning in their new home, "spake often one
to another," and established the means of grace.
The next step was to write urgent letters home asking
for a missionary to be sent. The appeal came up
for consideration at the Conference of 1842. While
the discussion on ways and means was going on,
Bottesford Circuit threw out the happy suggestion
that the Sunday School scholars of the Connexion
might sustain the Australian mission. About the
same time a memorable missionary meeting at
Cramlington in the North Shields Circuit enlarged
the project by suggesting that the Sunday School
teachers should undertake the charge of sending a
missionary to New Zealand. The idea was taken
up with enthusiasm and, after some little delay
caused by securing suitable agents, Messrs. Long
and Wilson arrived at Port Adelaide in October
1844. Six weeks before this, Robert Ward had
landed at New Plymouth, a stranger amongst
strangers—uninvited and unexpected. Taking him
all in all, Robert Ward must be regarded as satis-
fying the ideal of a pioneer colonial missionary.
To him more than to any other single man was due
the foundation work of New Zealand Primitive
Methodism.

Geographical Extension on a Larger Scale.—Thus,
just when in the old land geographical extension
seemed to have reached its limit, it began again and
on a much larger scale in Greater Britain. The
colonial pioneers had to do with distances dwarfing
those the pioneers at home had to cover. Think

of John Sharp, in 1857, having to travel 1,200 miles
to attend his District Meeting, and J. Buckle, of
Brisbane, speaking in 1863 of the neighbouring
Circuit of Rockhampton, 441 miles off ! Then, too,
the difficulties of pioneering in lands as yet un-
reclaimed from the wilderness require us to enlarge
our ideas of what " roughing it " means. As the
record of a single journey, we know nothing to equal
that taken by Robert Ward on his return from his
first visit to Auckland. He had a hundred miles
to go on foot—not on turnpike roads, but through
marsh and scrub, over rock-strewn beaches, and
mountain passes. Steady walking was varied now
by wading, and then by climbing. At night he
slept in native *pahs*, and once at least he and his
Maori guide lay on the sand. There were other
special difficulties besides the physical—difficulties
created by the sad interruption of the Maori war,
the gold-fever, and the constant shifting of the
population which often scattered the societies the
missionary had painfully gathered. No wonder
that the wear and tear was heavy in the early days ;
that some withdrew, broken in spirit or in health,
and that others were invalided home.

Colonial Missions in the Providential Order.—
Editor Petty, in an appeal written in 1855, speaks
" of the Connexion's manifest duty to our Colonies
abroad. We have not at present," he goes on to say,
" the means of engaging in a mission to the heathen,
but we have abundant means of engaging largely in
Colonial as well as in Home and City and Town

Missions. . . . *Oh, that we may know our mission,*
listen devoutly to the calls of Providence, and enter
fully those fields of usefulness to which we are
invited." It may be that the Connexion as a whole
was not fully awake to the designs of Providence,
and that even the executive at first dealt with the
Colonial Missions with a slack hand. But who, as
he sees what Canada, Australia, and New Zealand
have already grown to be, will not be thankful that
Primitive Methodism began early to do something to
ensure the stability, progress, and religious character
of these giant Commonwealths of the future ? We
cannot follow the progress of the Australian Missions
in detail. Some fine men, whose names are still
cherished in this country, were amongst the pioneer
workers—men such as Robert Hartley, John Sharp,
Michael Clark, E. C. Pritchard, and Joseph Warner.
In later years, Theophilus Parr, M.A., rendered
effective service, and John Watson, Hugh Gilmore
and J. D. Thompson, as the successive ministers of
South Adelaide Church, formed a sort of "Select
Preachership" and showed that Primitive Methodism
with its sympathy with Christian democracy had a
message that appealed to the emancipated and go-
ahead Antipodeans. When our Australian Churches
cast in their lot with the United Methodist
Church of Australia we parted with 11,683 members.
New Zealand elected to abide in connection with the
British Conference and did so until 1913.

III. A TIME OF TRANSITION: SOME NEW DEPARTURES.

" The old order changeth, yielding place to new,
And God fulfils Himself in many ways."
TENNYSON.

Superannuation and Death of our Founders.—The Conference of 1842 deemed it right to place both our chief founders on the retired list. As far back as 1827 William Clowes had been relieved of the care of a station. He was left free to labour as health and strength permitted. To him, therefore, official superannuation brought no great wrench. Far otherwise was it with Hugh Bourne, who, thanks to the abstemious habits of a lifetime, had much more physical vigour than his fellow-founder who was eight years his junior. After his superannuation William Clowes laid aside his " Journal," as though he had no further use for it ; but we know he kept the even tenor of his way and continued to preach as he was able ; that he was revered by his fellow-citizens and beloved by his own people who sought his counsels and counted his prayers a benediction. A final stroke of paralysis cut the thread of life, March 2nd, 1851, the sixtieth anniversary of Wesley's death-day. To Hugh Bourne superannuation was painful, but it meant a change rather than a stoppage of work. Though seventy-two years of age he volunteered to visit the Churches of Canada and the United States. The Conference of 1844 yielded to his urgent request with some misgivings, and before the Conference of 1846 he was back again, having gone through an amount of labour that might have taxed the strength of a man in his prime. Then he threw himself with ardour into the cause of temperance, travelling up and down preaching " Christian Temperance," advocating the " Golden System," and interesting himself in the welfare of the Churches he visited. October 11th, 1852, was Hugh Bourne's last day on earth. As the quiet autumnal evening fell, he awoke from his slumber on his couch in the Bemersley parlour. He seemed conscious of the presence of spirit-forms, and lifted his hand as if to greet them. Then with the words, " Old companions ! Old companions ! My mother ! " the brave soul passed from the way-worn suffering body.

General Missionary Committee Formed.—The clashing of thought, the competition of ideals, the free canvassing of all existing forms and institutions, that mark the decennium 1833–43 were fertile of results even so far as Primitive Methodism was concerned. Some changes had their inception in this seed-plot period which were to have far-reaching issues. These changes might be begun in a cautious, tentative way ; but they *were* begun—that was the great thing ; and they went on growing through the years, and Holborn Hall, and the General Missionary Committee of 1888 are the outcome of those beginnings. The later story of this evolution must be told further on. By the superannuation of the founders a devolution and distribution of administrative authority took place. The direction of affairs fell into more, and younger, hands. For years Hugh Bourne had attended most of the District Meetings as General Committee Delegate. To a limited extent his brother James and William Clowes had shared in these official appointments. Now, seven men were deputed to attend the seven District Meetings of 1843. Among the appointees were the coming Connexional officers—the men of the Transition we may call them—Thomas Holliday, John and William Garner, and John Flesher, by right of eminence their chief. Without the shadow of a doubt he was the greatest and most influential figure of this decennium. John Flesher had been asked by the Conference of 1841, " aided by any of the brethren, to put into legislative form his thoughts relative to a Connexional Missionary Committee." The outcome of this was the thorough reorganisation of the Committee which had nominally existed since 1823, but whose operations had been on a very limited scale; confined, indeed—after John Petty's early and remarkable mission to Pembrokeshire—to rendering occasional help to the Circuits in carrying on their missions. Now, as a beginning, Hull handed over its missions to the Committee. To these were added Oswestry's Lisburn mission. John Garner, " a moderate Conservative in church matters," as his brother William calls him, was appointed the Committee's General Secretary, and Thomas Holliday, the Assistant Book Steward, was appointed Treasurer. The missions were, until the formation of the London District in 1853, attached to Hull District. A room

G

twelve feet square on the Book Room premises became the Connexion's modest Mission House. The forward step thus taken was regarded as an experimental one and was not taken without some misgivings. The new measures launched were optional rather than compulsory. The old method went on for some years side by side with the new. In 1844 the number of Circuit Missions was in excess of those under the care of the Committee—35 to 27. Not till 1862 were the last two Circuit Missions, Bromyard and Falmouth, taken over. The dual system thus obtaining is a further proof that the period of which we write was a Transition one. It took some years to pass from Circuit to Connexional missions, from an indefinite number of managing committees to one strong executive. It took just a generation (1876) before the Committee could boldly say : " We have had enough of fractions. Henceforth you must remit the *whole* of your missionary money to us. You are not a Circuit else—only a mission disguised."

Removal of the Book Room to London.—Nor was this the only change effected in 1843. In January of that year John Flesher took up the office of Editor which Hugh Bourne had held since 1820. A short experience served to convince him that a change of location was inevitable, that Bemersley was no longer a suitable place at which the Connexion's " central wheel of management " should revolve. On the ground of efficiency, convenience and economy, and also to escape local embarrassments and secure greater freedom of action, it was,

he believed, indispensable to change the location of
the Book Room and the Connexional executive.
John Flesher got his way ; the Conference of 1843
accepted his views, and the move—no light matter
in those days—was made to St. George's in the East,
where the Book Room and Mission headquarters
were located side by side. The shifting of the
Connexion's centre from a Staffordshire hamlet to
London, with its then two million of inhabitants,
registered the changes which the years had brought
about. Now, the Connexion was no longer a rural
rather than an urban movement, or mainly confined
to the Midlands and the North. Our leaders fore-
saw that for years to come mission work must be
resolutely pushed in the South and in London—
itself a province. Further, it is clear that by 1843
we must have got a promising foothold in London,
or the "central wheel of management" would not
have been set up within its radius. How, then,
did Primitive Methodism get to London, and what
was its position there in 1843–53 ? These questions
the next section must briefly endeavour to answer.

IV. LONDON PRIMITIVE METHODISM TO 1853.

"London is London still, careless, trifling, gay, and hardened
through the deceitfulness of sin. . . . Oh, for God's mighty
arm to be outstretched to shake the mighty Babylon to its centre."
                              WILLIAM CLOWES, 1824.

*Leeds Circuit takes up the Work of Missioning
London.*—The story of how Primitive Methodism
was introduced to London* properly belongs to the

---

* John Benton had laboured a short time in London in 1811.

Probation Period of our history—the period of
unlimited faith and limited means. But it is told
here in order to keep like things together and preserve due sequence. It might fittingly be called
"The Story of Two Winters' Days." In December
1822, Leeds Circuit, finding itself forestalled in
missioning Sunderland, turned its attention to
London and sent Paul Sugden and Thomas Watson
to be its missionaries. When the coach drew up at
" The Swan with Two Necks " the last shilling of
the two travellers went as a tip to the coachman.
To the guard, who also touched his hat expectantly,
Sugden artlessly explained how matters stood—
who they were, what their errand, and their absolute
pennilessness. The guard was a Christian man,
and a discerning one withal, who knew guilelessness
when he saw it. He took the missionaries home,
gave them breakfast, and bought a hymn-book to
help keep starvation at bay. That guard was one
of the anonymous benefactors of our early time and
doubtless will not fail of his reward. A kind Providence watched over these two " frae the North," for
they found temporary relief in working for the
Bible Christians. Watson by " a peculiar chain
of circumstances " discovered a helpful co-religionist,
and next day a small quaint meeting-house in
Bethnal Green was taken on rent. Soon Watson,
who was an unpaid evangelist, had to return to
Leeds, and Paul Sugden was left in sole charge of
the London mission. Late in January, 1823, John
Coulson made his entry into London with three
shillings in his pocket. He had walked from Leeds

and had no address in London to make for ; a vague idea that the chapel was in the neighbourhood of old Shoreditch Church was all he had to guide him.   As he made his way along the streets, in the simplicity of his faith he prayed, " Lord, it would be a little thing with Thee to let me meet with Paul Sugden." And he *did* meet with him.   As he was passing a shop Brother Sugden ran out to greet his newly-arrived colleague. This timely coincidence was rightly regarded as " of the Lord's doing." One cannot but linger over these incidents in which one finds a *sancta simplicitas* recalling the best traditions of the palmy days of the Franciscans.

Hull Circuit takes over the Mission, 1824.—Hull Circuit's chief missionary, William Clowes, made his entry into London January 1824, and laboured there for a year and eight months.   Wherever Clowes was doing pioneer work things were sure to happen—things worth calling " incidents," and worth recording.   So it was with Clowes in London. Some of his strange experiences on this arduous mission he has related in his published Journal. Yet, notwithstanding his zeal and incessant labours during these twenty months, he has to confess " the chariot rolled on slowly and heavily." William Clowes had not been used to so slow an advance.   When he left London for Cornwall in September 1825, there were only 170 members in society.   Yet another change !   From 1828 to 1834 London formed part of the Norwich District. Then it disappears from the stations, the explanation

being that the London Circuit had got into difficulties
and was again taken under the wing of Hull Circuit.
Humanly speaking, John Flesher was the saviour
of London Primitive Methodism. For what might
have seemed a forlorn-hope, Hull gave up its best
man. Mr. Flesher heroically endeavoured to save
Blue Gate Fields Chapel, built in 1832. He
travelled hither and thither in the Connexion in its
behalf. Thomas Watson, the boy-preacher, wore
out three suits of clothes in begging for the distressed chapel ! But in the end it had to be sold
for £500, and nothing was saved but Connexional
honour and faith and courage. In 1837 we had
only 286 members, and not a shilling's worth of
Connexional property in London ; for Cooper's
Gardens second chapel was the private property of
John Friskin, who let it to the friends at an easy
rental. In 1838, the lease of land and cottages
near Commercial Road was bought. John Flesher
borrowed the money, was architect, clerk of the
works, and, if tradition speaks truly, often brick-
layer's labourer as well. It may safely be said he
built Sutton Street Chapel. Primitive Methodism
in London was saved. From this time the tide
turned, and never since has it seriously ebbed. In
1847, after John Ride's three years' labours, London
had 700 members and three Connexional chapels—
Cooper's Gardens (which had been purchased),
Sutton Street, and Grove Mews, Marylebone.
Besides these, old " Elim " in Fetter Lane had been
taken on rent in 1845 and continued in occupation
till the 'seventies. The six years of George Austin's

superintendency were years of progress. The societies were again formed into a Circuit, while Hammersmith became a mission. When, in 1853, London became the head of a new District, it had three Circuits—Cooper's Gardens, Sutton Street, and Elim.

John Flesher's Retirement.—In 1852—the year of Hugh Bourne's death—John Flesher, his legitimate official successor, was superannuated ; but not before there stood to his credit a goodly record of achievements. He had prepared, on very original lines, the Consolidated Minutes of 1849, wherein will be found a plan and rules for a Middle-class School. He had drawn up (1852) an elaborate report on a proposed Equalisation Fund, in which he favours the district system afterwards adopted. Of the Hymn Book of 1853 which he compiled we have already spoken. He was admittedly the most cultivated and admired preacher of the denomination during tHis Transition Period. Our fathers were thrifty in their words of praise, even when the outgoing Editor was John Flesher. So in a printed resolution it stands recorded : " We are satisfied with the way in which brother John Flesher has discharged his duties." If the brethren were satisfied, the retiring Editor was probably satiated ; for in that yeasty time the office he had filled was no sinecure, as the papers that have passed through our hands clearly show. He had earned his rest. In his retirement he could thankfully reflect that " whilst it was never my policy to start divisions and disturbances, it was often my work to have to allay them when raging, and to deprive them to a certain extent of the power of a resurrection." The witness is true. Not merely did he pilot the London cause through its crisis. He stood in the breach at Hull during the Stamp troubles of 1841 and, earlier still (1830), he had gone to Edinburgh to save the situation.

Behind the Fluctuations of the Annual Numerical Returns there is history confirmatory of what has been said of a Church's sensitiveness to the happenings, the main currents and tendencies of the time. The largest increase our Church has reported hitherto, occurred in this period. The *Cholera morbus* is behind this increase of 9,205 for 1850. Statistics show that in 1848 and 1849 53,293 persons died in England and Wales of that scourge. This stimulated many of the churches, especially in the large towns, to greater activity, and predisposed the people to receive the Gospel. On the other hand, the aggregate decrease of 4,126 for the three years 1853–5 has behind it the gold-fever, the depletion of many Circuits by emigration, the Crimean War, the unprecedented storms and floods which devastated many parts of East Anglia, the high price of food and commodities. Above all, we must allow for the indirect results of the Wesleyan Reform agitation. We studiously endeavoured to preserve a strict neutrality during these years of ecclesiastical strife, but all experience goes to show that, do as they will, neutrals often fall in for more than their dues of loss and discomfort. And so these two decades of perturbation and change ended, appropriately enough by a Fast and Day of Prayer being observed throughout the Connexion.

It was not so, however, when the Jubilee Year was reached. For the fourth time an increase of over eight thousand was reported. Here, again, we look behind the tabular returns and this time we see the Irish Revival and the quickening influence which, going forth from it, had reached so many English Churches. We had some part in that great Revival, were it only that Richard Jukes' hymns, such as " Christ for me," " What's the News ? " and " Mercy's Free," had such a vogue throughout the revival. But great Revivals were no uncommon thing in this period. In 1909 a writer whose age and wide experience carries weight wrote, "Apart from Primitive Methodism there was little revivalism for some years before 1859." He affirms that from the beginning Richard Jukes' had been a revivalistic ministry, and, as such, was according to type, and he emphasises the influence of his hymns.* Some of the great revivals of this period have become historic, like the one in Allendale, 1859–60, under C. C. M'Kechnie. As we read in the biographies of Thomas Batty, John Petty and Parkinson Milson of these times of ingathering we long for their return. At the Jubilee Conference of 1860 the membership stood at 132,114, and there was an increase in every department. No wonder it was pronounced " a good Conference " and that the seventy-seven brethren who composed it set their faces to the future with a good heart.

* Rev. W. Mottram in *The British Weekly*, June 17th, 1909.

V. The Jubilee Commemoration and the Sense of the Past.

" Let us now praise famous men, and our fathers that begat us."

Ecclesiasticus xliv. 1.

The net monetary results of the Jubilee Celebrations were disappointingly small, and we may be inclined to wonder and ask for the balance-sheet. But no ; the financial aspect of the Jubilee stirs only a languid interest now. Let us pass on. What most concerns us is to ask—What did the Jubilee year do in giving the Connexion *a heightened sense and a firmer hold of its past ?* There is need for caution here lest we unconsciously carry back to 1860 thoughts and feelings that have required another half-century of Connexional life to deepen. The Connexion was still young in 1860, and thought of the dead pretty much as the young think of *their* departed—of the few particular friends who have gone from sight and hearing, rather than of " the great multitude." The populousness of the spirit-world is not brought home to them as it is to the old ; these are made to realise that the friends they have in the beyond outnumber those who are still left to them. All in good time ! We must not confuse the standpoints of the Jubilee and the Centenary. Still, there is evidence to show that by 1860 Primitive Methodism was becoming more alive to the fact that it had a past to remember and be proud of, as well as a future to make. This sentiment—this datum of consciousness—was naturally not much in evidence in the early part of this period ; though we can discover it struggling to express itself in the Conference Resolution of 1833 which required that henceforth the number of deaths in each Circuit must be annually reported. This was accordingly done for the first time in 1834. This regulation was not made on the initiative of the Conference, but at the solicitation of the people— under pressure in fact. The feeling of the Connexion's solidarity with its past was nascent—the feeling that we ought not to lose touch with our departed ; that we should number them as still belonging to us. This " sense of the past " was stirred and strengthened by the comparatively recent deaths of William Clowes and Hugh Bourne, and now, further, by the protracted and widespread Jubilee celebrations. Those who assembled at the Tunstall Conference of 1860, or took part in the Camp Meetings and great public gatherings that were held throughout the Connexion, were made aware they were in no mean succession, and already had an inspiring history and rich traditions. All this is a great asset to any Church. Thomas Church, the London layman, was a diligent user of the pen in the interests of the Connexion. He issued many books and pamphlets all designed to familiarise our people with their own history, to help them to realise that there had been bequeathed to them a goodly heritage, with the condition annexed of handing it down unimpaired and enlarged to succeeding generations. And now that the Jubilee had come, a goodly number of writers sought to recall the

Connexion's past and emphasise our " obligations
to the dead."   The venerable John Petty's official
" History of the Primitive Methodist Connexion "
still deservedly holds high rank in this special form
of literature.   Nor must William Garner's " Life
of the Venerable William Clowes " and his " Jubilee
of English Camp Meetings " be forgotten.

CHAPTER VII

The "Connexion" in Mid-Victorian Days: 1860-85.

" A dozen or two—really indeed more like hundreds—of splendid life-histories go to every little bit of the task of finding the track or building up the fabric."

BERNARD BOSANQUET, F.B.A.

I. ROUGH-HEWING ITS FUTURE.

The Connexion Goes into Committee.—When we excavate the old Minutes of Conference relating to the period we now enter upon, we somehow get the impression that the entire Connexion had gone into Committee during these years, and even beyond them. The impression leaves us rather confused and, it may be, slightly taken aback. It is only when we turn away from the endless committees sitting and reporting, and fasten on what was the tendency and outcome of it all, that we experience a measure of relief. Any touch of impatience prompting the question : " Why were the fathers so long making up their minds in regard to missions and other vital matters ? " may be checked by the thought that our fathers' motto seems to have been " Make haste slowly." Often had they to do what they could, rather than what they would.

Most things that last, whether they be trees or institutions or churches, do grow that way. Indeed no other way was open to our predecessors than this. The Connexion was slowly and cautiously orienting itself. The fathers were the pathfinders. They were blazing a track through the forest ; finding the right direction across the moor. If it had not been for their pioneer efforts we should not have got where we are to-day.

Position of the Conference and the Districts in this Period.—As we watch the tendencies at work we see that they must end—as they do—in the gradual elevation of the Conference and the lowering in prestige of the Districts. Towards the end of the period we notice that the Conference has grown in numbers and in much else. It has ceased to shroud itself in mystery ; it even welcomes reporters and courts publicity. The restrictions with which it hedged itself round have either been repealed or allowed to become a dead letter. The chief officer of the Conference is becoming a much more important functionary than he was formerly. You used to have to search the Minutes to find out who actually had been the President for a given year. Now his name stands at the head of the Connexional officers. Once he may have been only the Chairman of the last day's sessions who signed the Conference Journal ; now he is on his way to become the President for the year and for the entire Connexion. As for the District Synods as we may call them— for the evolution proceeds on Presbyterial lines—

they may be more in number ; but they are in some cases smaller than they were because of the partition of the Districts. But the Conference enlarges as the Connexion itself enlarges. This may be made apparent by figures. In 1832 the Conference was made up of thirty-one representatives ; in 1860 of seventy-seven ; in 1885 of one hundred and eighty-six. But all abatements notwithstanding, Districtism continued to flourish until the levelling of the District boundaries in 1879, and the " District man " was its peculiar product. Now, the District man is gone never to return. District " sectionalism " might be an undesirable thing ; but it had its strong points. The District barriers enclosed garden-plots in which ideas could be cultivated—ideas that ultimately commended themselves as suitable for transplantation, and *were* transplanted accordingly, to the great advantage of the Connexion. Such nurseries were Leeds District with its home-growths of the Chapel Fund and the Sunday School Union, and markedly by Norwich District where, as early as the 'thirties, the idea of sending missionaries to Africa was nursed and propagated. The first African missionary meeting was held at Swaffham in 1852. Thomas Low, the minister, author of " The Pilot of the Gallilean Lake," and James Fuller, the layman, were " gone on Africa," it was said. Nor were they alone by any means ; and no amount of cold water could damp their enthusiasm. At length their persistency was rewarded, as we shall presently see.

II.　Ministerial Training and Educational Matters.

Imperfect Co-ordination of Culture and Evangelism.
—What is the right relation that should subsist between Culture and Church-life was a vexed, much controverted question at the beginning of this period. The views held were opposed and often came in conflict. The fact thus barely stated should be understood ; for it could be enlarged upon at great length and confirmed by copious references to printed and documentary evidence— were it but worth while. To learn what were the views of the minority—strong in everything save numbers—we have only to look into the first volume of " The Christian Ambassador," and read the two opening articles. John Lightfoot writes : " As the disadvantages endured by Primitive Methodist ministers generally produce in them a painful consciousness of their comparative inability to meet the demands of the times for a higher tone of intellectuality and spiritual power, this Publication has been originated by a few of them in the Northern District." Then Thomas Greenfield writes in a more cheerful vein : " It cannot fail to strike us that there is, at present, a growing demand for an intellectual, or, in other words, an educated ministry." There *was ;* but the demand had to reckon with a good deal of *vis inertiæ* and prejudice and even stout opposition. The battle was joined on the question of establishing an institution for the training of accepted candidates for the ministry.

Elmfield School and our first Theological Institutes.
—As far back as 1844, John Gordon Black of
Sunderland had mooted at the Lynn Conference
the desirability of starting a ministerial college ;
but the suggestion was crushed as one would crush
" that fly." Even the saintly and scholarly John
Petty, writing a Jubilee paper in the Magazine of
1860 could say : " Unquestionably the great body of
our people would look upon such an institution
with disapproval, if not with jealousy and alarm,"
and express his preference for an arrangement
by which young men should be trained under
experienced ministers. And yet, five years had not
passed before the writer of these words found himself
installed as first Principal of a Theological Institute
as well as Governor of Elmfield School ! Even
before the Jubilee accounts were finally closed and
the decision made that one-third of the proceeds
of the Fund should be divided equally between
the School and ministerial training, Elmfield House
had been acquired. The building was reconstructed
in 1864, the school started and, in September 1865,
eight ministerial students were already in residence.
The business seems to have been skilfully piloted
and must have had some long-headed and strong-
willed men at the back of it. We seem to discern
astuteness too in the choice and size of the
Committee—of ninety members—appointed as a
Committee of " ways and means." Another Committee was named in 1866 to look out for a suitable
building for a ministerial College. The old In-
firmary at Sunderland was selected and altered to
H

meet its new requirements. In 1868 Principal
Petty died, from overwork it is to be feared, and in
1869 the Conference listened to Dr. William Antliff
giving his first report of the Sunderland Theological
Institute. The cause of ministerial training had
to pass through choppy seas during the rest of this
period. Manchester College was opened in 1881.
The times were unpropitious : for a brief while
there were two Colleges, neither of them half-filled,
and then another brief while when both stood
empty. But the period of depression passed, and
Manchester College was reopened in 1883 with
James Macpherson as its Principal. The evolution
of Manchester College into "Hartley College"
belongs to a subsequent period. As for the Sunderland Institute, its after fortunes can be told in a
few words. After having acted for some time as
Tutor, Thomas Greenfield, on the retirement of
Dr. William Antliff, was appointed Principal. Last
stage of all, the building itself was disposed of and
the net proceeds of the sale given to the funds
of Manchester College. ELMFIELD COLLEGE under
the Governorships of Thomas Smith (obit. 1879)
and Robert Smith (1880–5) and a succession of
able Head Masters, went forward prosperously.
BOURNE COLLEGE, QUINTON, a younger Elmfield
planted in the busy Midlands, was opened in 1882,
with G. Middleton, F.G.S., as its Governor and
J. S. Hooson, M.A., as its Head Master. A Conference Committee appointed in 1885 reported of
both these Colleges : " They are doing a great work
for the future of Primitive Methodism." It was a

disappointment to many that when Elmfield College was begun, contrary to expectations, no provision was made for the higher education of girls. To supply the omission a limited liability company was formed and a HIGH SCHOOL FOR GIRLS established at Clapham, S.E., with Rev. William Rowe as its Principal. It began under what seemed' encouraging auspices. But its life was a brief one—its last report will be found in the Minutes of 1881—and the company was wound up. Primitive Methodism has had its DAY SCHOOLS, too, but they have been the outcome of local enterprise and not a Connexional institution. Much discussion went on in the Conference and elsewhere in the 'sixties on the desirability or otherwise of making the Day School an integral part of our organisation. No one will be surprised at this who is acquainted with the fearful state of things prevailing at the time with regard to elementary school education.* The Connexion would have been callous indeed if anxiety on this subject had not found voice in its highest court. But there was the vexed question of government grants ; and on that question opinion was pretty equally divided—so much so, that the Conference of 1868 decided " to leave every station at liberty to use its own discretion in applying for such aid." Yet the very next year, the writer of the Conference Address to the Churches devotes a stirring paragraph to the subject : " The Day School should

---

* " In 1869 it was realised that, if England was to survive as a great nation, childhood must be saved. . . . The state of things was indeed fearful."—*The Quarterly Review*, Oct. 1917.

become one of our great Connexional institutions."
He even sees the time coming when "it may be
found requisite to provide a Normal School whence
shall be supplied competent teachers to take charge
of our schools." Next year Mr. Forster brought
in his famous Education Bill and the situation was
completely changed.

Guarding the Gate to the Ministry.—Primitive
Methodist preachers are, to begin with, a much
examined class. When and how did the system
have its rise ?   We must go back to 1854 to find its
beginnings.   The Conference of that year had to
deal with several painful cases of ministerial in-
efficiency ; whereupon James Macpherson carried
a resolution instructing the General Committee
"to prepare some legislation for effectually testing
the efficiency of candidates for the ministry, either
on entering or closing their probation." (Here let
it be remembered of Mr. Macpherson to his honour,
that for years he was the unpaid director of the
studies of the young preachers of the Manchester
District.) The General Committee fulfilled its
commission, and 1855 ushered in the era of
examinations which, until the late 'sixties, were
oral and not written.   And when written examinations based on text-books did begin, the first
examination of the kind, in 1868, had this peculiarity,
that adjectives and not figures were used to value
the papers. A meter of values was adopted,
descending from "excellent" and "very good"
down to "indifferent" and "bad," and the results

read out to the whole District Meeting. No good purpose would be served by trying to unravel the tangled mass of legislation that somehow has brought us to the highly developed system that now obtains. The point to notice is that " How can we best secure fitness in our rising ministry ? " was deemed a question of vital importance and—a knotty one.

Connexional Sunday School Union, 1874.—Had a Sunday School Union been established forty years earlier than it was it would not have been an un-timely birth. Such an institution would have embodied one of the ruling ideas of Hugh Bourne, just as the Camp Meeting and Book Room did. It would have come in the way of natural sequence. In the Consolidated Minutes of 1832 it is asked : " What may be done respecting Sunday Schools and Tracts ? ANSWER : Let a P.M. Sunday School Union be formed and Tracts printed as soon as well may be." Here we have two of the chief interests of our founder as a practical idealist linked together : the spiritual welfare of the young, and the circulation of the printed word as an effective agency. It is an ideal to be kept in view and worked for. It might seem that Hugh Bourne's charge, " Take care of the children," was not taken up with the enthusiasm that burnt so steadily in him. As a whole the Connexion did not light its candle at his flame. We have said " on the whole " this was so. For a number of years all we have in the Minutes of Conference is the aggregate number of Sunday Schools, teachers and scholars, gathered from the

Circuit reports. But there were local candles
burning, and these showed the way. In Leeds
first Circuit a Sunday School Union was formed
under such men at Mr. G. W. Armitage (the nephew
of the well-known minister of the same name) and
Mr. William Beckworth. The Union comprised six
schools within a radius of ten miles, and it held
its first Annual Tea Meeting on January 2nd, 1858.
A few years later Mr. Armitage removed to Manchester and there helped to form a Sunday School
Union on a still larger scale, embracing as it did
several Circuits. A report of this Union appeared
in the Magazine, January 1867. Two different
Committees sat in 1872–3 to consider the subject
in all its bearings, and the second Committee was
instructed "to forward the result of its deliberations
to the various District Committees and thereafter
to the Conference of 1874." After all this very
deliberate and cautious procedure, that Conference
" re-affirmed the principle " of a Sunday School
Union. Joseph Wood was appointed as its secretary
and organiser : the next year he was set apart to
the work, which had its executive at Leeds. There
is no doubt the work before the Secretary was
arduous and exacting ; and assuredly Joseph
Wood, a strong personality, was just the man for so
difficult a post. As Mr. Beckworth says : " There
was not the necessary enthusiasm at first to carry
the Union beyond the voluntary stage, but a few
years later it had so won its way to confidence that
it was then felt safe to make the enrolment of every
school compulsory." The aims of the Union—to

be ever kept in view and steadily worked for—were never perhaps more clearly defined than in the Union's second Annual Report in 1876 : " To benefit the schools in every possible way—in their equipment and management, and productiveness—to incorporate them more fully with our various Connexional Institutions, and *weld them into vital union with the Church, sharing in her life and affording a principal field for her activity.*"* But the drawers up of the Report were under no illusions : the road to the goal, they knew, was a long and uphill one, and caution and patience would be needed. The organisation of the Union has been gradually extended and improved. In 1877 catechumen classes were established. 1879 was a productive year : it saw the creation of District Sunday School Committees, the publication of the first Sunday School Hymn Book, prepared by Dr. G. Booth and Mr. William Beckworth, which served our schools for twenty-one years. It saw, too, the beginnings of Temperance and Band of Hope work " under Connexional supervision." Band of Hope members were first reported in 1880 : from 38,774 in that year they had by 1885 grown to 92,512.

Defective Co-ordination was a marked general characteristic of the Mid-Victorian period. Of this the capital example is, of course, the arrogant attitude of science to religion in those days as represented by Tyndall, Huxley and Clifford ; and the stand-off, suspicious attitude of Religion to

* The italics are ours.

Science. As Bernard Bosanquet has recently written : " The disconnection of things is a Philistine and a pessimistic doctrine." If that be true, then " The Philistine Period" would not be an inapt designation of the mid-years of Victoria's reign. Once more, the Churches—not excluding our own—did not escape the prevailing tendency of the times. In our own Church we have seen the tendency at work in the difficulties which had to be evaded or overcome before an institution for the training of ministers could be established. We meet with the same phenomenon in the Connexion's slowness to take its part in sending missionaries into purely heathen lands ; and in the lower particularist motives which made the " invitation system," and establishment of a strong Sunday School Union practically co-extensive with the Connexion, a work of time. In each of these cases the victory was with the progressive life of the Connexion ; but with what an expenditure of time and toil and anxiety was the victory purchased ! But, " It is not thy duty to complete the work ; but neither art thou free to desist from it."

III.   OUR FIRST MISSIONS IN AFRICA.

" *Where Afric's Sunny Fountains roll down their golden sand.*"—As early as 1837, Joseph Diboll, a Yarmouth shoemaker, pleaded the cause of Africa at the Sheffield Conference. Finding no door of access to Africa through his own Church, Joseph

Diboll sought another door elsewhere. But the Norwich District ever kept the cause of African Missions in view and took care that it should be brought before the Connexion as well. At last a definitive step was taken at the Jubilee Conference of 1860 : the Connexion as a whole became committed to the African Mission " as soon as suitable men could be found." Amongst the delegates sat Thomas Low, W. Lift, and James Fuller. It was a high, proud moment for them and the District they represented. But, strange to say, a year and eight months had to elapse before the right men were found, and R. W. Burnett and Henry Roe set sail in the " Mandingo," January 25th, 1870. The causes of this strange retardment have probably been glanced at in the preceding section.

The Objective of the African Mission Changed.— For years the eyes of the Connexion had been fixed on the *continent* of Africa, and especially on Natal, as the sphere of the contemplated mission. The platform and printing-press had familiarised our people with the name, the physical features, and many advantages of the Colony. Yet, by one of those strange turns of events which sometimes occur, the unexpected happened. The first foreign mission was not planted on the Continent of Africa, but on a small island off its west coast—Fernando Po in the Bight of Biafra. On a certain day in August 1869, the ship " Elgiva " dropped her anchor and remained some days off Santa Isabel. The master of this ship, Capt. W. Robinson, and

ship-carpenter James Hands, were both Primitive
Methodists belonging to the Liverpool second
Circuit. Finding that, though the Baptist missionaries had quitted the island the year before, the
little flock left behind had not lost its relish for
divine things, they tried to break to it the Word
of Life. They sang and prayed, and ship-carpenter
Hands preached to the people and won their hearts.
A requisition from the island thus visited by godly
laymen was forwarded to England praying that
missionaries might be sent. The requisition bore
the date August 28th, 1869, and on the 21st February,
1870, the " Mandingo," with the first missionaries
on board, cast her anchor. In this entirely natural
way—by laymen first, plying their calling, and
followed by missionaries—was Primitive Methodism
planted in Africa.

A Costly but Productive Mission.—No doubt,
judged by the money standard, Fernando Po has
been a costly mission. Its unfavourable climatic
conditions have resulted in much human wear and
tear and necessitated frequent changes in the staff.
Missionaries like R. S. Blackburn—our first standard-
bearer to fall on heathen soil—and M. H. Barron ;
and missionaries' wives like Mrs. Maylott and
Mrs. Boocock—have given their lives for Fernando
Po. And, although Mr. and Mrs. Luddington
did not die on African soil, they were so broken
in health after three terms of service that they
both died soon after their return to England. Then,
again and again, the educational and evangelistic

work of our agents has been interrupted and even stopped by some Spanish governor amenable to priestly influence. W. Holland was banished, and W. Welford was for a time put in durance. Twice over the General Missionary Secretary of the time has had to travel to Madrid to try to straighten out the tangle. Strong drink has been another serious impediment to success. The traders' greed of gain in pitting rum against the Gospel has doubled the missionaries' difficulties. We put the contra case strongly. But material profit and loss and spiritual returns are incommensurable : they cannot be weighed in the same scales. That truth flashes out in the declaration of D. T. Maylott : " If the Fernando Po mission had done nothing more than effect the conversion and training of W. N. Barley-corn, it would still be a glorious success." Boldly may it be affirmed that Fernando Po has done much for our people. It has served to nurture the missionary spirit, even more perhaps than an easier, quick-returns mission might have done. It has been a school for the training of missionaries and a stepping-stone to the regions beyond. It is note-worthy that in the same year our missionaries landed in Fernando Po, 1870, Henry Buckenham opened a mission at Aliwal North on the continent of Africa itself—though not in Natal. It was also by invitation that this now well-known and extensive station was planted. Mr. Buckenham's successors, reaching slightly beyond our period, were John Smith, (two terms) and John (afterwards Dr.) Watson. The names of Henry Buckenham and John Smith,

both Norwich District men, link us on to the next
period, when we shall see a notable development of
missionary enterprise.

IV   THE CLOSE OF A DISTINCTLY-MARKED PERIOD.

A Year of Endings and Beginnings.—1885 was,
Connexionally, a notable year in this regard. We
have now specially to do with the period's terminals.
The distinction made is not a chronological one
merely, accorded it because just a quarter of a century
had elapsed since the Jubilee. The distinction
belongs to it of right, because it rounded off another
lap in the Connexion's course and brought a well-
defined period to a close.

The Passing of Districtism.—First and chief of all :
Districtism, the peculiar product of a given time,
received its death-blow. It might still linger a
few years, but it could never again be what it had
been. It was " positively the last time " that the
twenty-four delegates of the wide Sunderland District,
elected on a numerical basis, would come up to
Conference in full strength. The District was
divided into three, and an era of partition swiftly
set in, by which some anomalies of representation
were removed and some approach made to equal
electoral areas. Besides accomplishing this, there
were grounds for hoping that the readjustments
made would reduce expenditure, tend to convenience,
and perhaps bring a greater number and variety

of talents into use—which, Hugh Bourne maintained,
should always be kept in view.

The Passing of a Cloud from the Connexional Sky
was also another feature of 1885. The temporarily
clouded prospect was largely due to external causes.
The late 'seventies was a time of severe commercial
depression in this and other lands which adversely
affected the interests of the Connexion, especially
the Missionary Society and our heavily burdened
chapel property. Besides what came from without,
there was a cause operating from within—the
natural effect (human nature being what it is) of the
enactment of 1876 which required the whole of the
missionary money raised on the Circuits to be
remitted to the General Treasurer. These causes
together led to a decline year by year in missionary
revenue until, by 1880, there was a deficit on the
current account of £5,000. A remedy was sought.
Legislation was sent up ; Committees sat. Some
of the best brains in the Connexion were deep in
consultation as to what was best to be done to
brighten the outlook. The venerable James Travis
has given us the inside history of this time—and he
knows ; for he was the parent, and not merely the
sponsor, of the legislation on the radical reform of
the General Missionary Committee which bore fruit
in the next period. In 1885, Mr. W. P. Hartley—
not yet Sir William—steps to the front as a beneficent figure. He was chairman of the Metropolitan
Tabernacle Missionary meeting that year, and gave
£1,000 towards the liquidation of the constricting

debt. It was swept away. " Financial relief came like a vivifying breath." " Now," said John Atkinson, the new Secretary, " the debt is dead, buried, and without prospect of a resurrection." Reading Conference was like a junction in a great railway-system. It had lines running into it, and it had lines running from it. Though it is the convergent rather than the radiating lines that now concern us, yet we cannot but notice what is foreshadowed in the Conference Address of 1885 : " The Conference has resolved to enter new fields, and ' to attempt great things for God, and expect great things from God.' . . . The Conference has determined that an effort shall be made to deal with chapel debts."

Parting with the Churches in Canada.—In 1884, with the expression of hearty good-will on both sides, the daughter Church of Canada left us to become part of the great Methodist Church of the Dominion. In parting we surrendered 8,223 members, ninety-nine travelling and 246 local preachers, and 237 chapels. Yet, after " cutting " these losses, the numerical returns for 1885 gave the number of ministers at 1,042, lay preachers 15,785, Connexional chapels 4,282, and members 192,389. Comparing these figures with those of 1860, the net increase for the twenty-five years is seen to be 60,275.

The Passing of some Notable Figures significantly closes our period. Two pre-eminently " Connexional men " finished their long course almost together ;

the one six months before the Reading Conference, the other eight months after. William Antliff, D.D., and George Lamb both began their ministry in 1830 and rose to their representative position in the yeasty, transitional period which followed. Both had filled important offices, had twice been elected President of Conference, and been made members of the Deed Poll while still in the active ministry. Perhaps no one had attended more Conferences than Dr. W. Antliff, or possessed a more intimate knowledge of the Connexion—its men and its movements—except it may have been Hugh Bourne, and we are not sure that even he was an exception. The two veterans were both men of fine physique, though of different builds. Dr. Antliff might shine more in Conference debate or on the platform; but George Lamb had the ear of Conference, as of every business gathering, by virtue of his amiability, his probity and well-known soundness of judgment. He justified the confidence reposed in him when, being sent as a deputation to Canada at a critical time, he discharged his duties to the satisfaction of all. Moreover his business ability was shown in his administration of the Book Room (1865–70) and of important Circuits like Hull, in which town he ministered twenty years, preaching with all the old evangelical fervour, and visiting his flock almost up to the day of his death. He " ceased at once to work and live," February 13th, 1886, having travelled fifty-seven years.

CHAPTER VIII.

Maturing Church-Life: Various Manifestations, 1885-1897.

" From Whom the Body, in all its parts nourished and strengthened by its points of contact and its connexions, grows with a divine growth."

COL. II. 19 (Weymouth's rendering).

I. A BRIEF CONSPECTUS OF THE PERIOD.

Some Convenient Date-Marks.—The period begins, all but a day, with the defeat of Mr. Gladstone's Government. It ends with the year of Queen Victoria's Diamond Jubilee celebrations, the Conference of that year sending up a loyal Address to the Throne on the auspicious occasion. Representatives of the Connexion took their part in the impressive National Thanksgiving in front of St. Paul's. Ecclesiastically the Period ends with the launching of the National Council of the Evangelical Free Churches in which our denominational leaders took an active part. These reminders will fix the limits of the Period in the memory; also they naturally lead us to notice

The Change in the External Relations of the Denomination.—By this time we are struck with the remarkable change which had come about in the relations of Primitive Methodism to the larger life —political, social and especially ecclesiastical— around it. By 1832 Primitive Methodism had got through her own probation ; but the Churches and the outside public insisted upon putting her through another, and a much longer, probation, for their own satisfaction and assurance. That, too, was now ended ; and we were accepted in a fashion ; not enthusiastically, it may be, but we *were* accepted. It is an index-finger pointing to the change of sentiment that in the volume of the ninth edition of the " Encyclopædia Britannica" published in June 1885, what is said of Primitive Methodism is in striking contrast with what was said by some ill-instructed scribe in the eighth edition of 1857. There we are given the nickname of Belper minting, and our founders are contemptuously spoken of as " having separated themselves from the Wesleyan body because sufficient zeal was not manifested in obtruding religion upon the minds of the people." There is no stuff of this kind in Dr. Rigg's article of June 1885. We there get the name rightly belonging to us, and are thus described : " It has been a very successful body, aiming simply at doing evangelistic work, and is now numerous and powerful, numbering among its ministers not only many useful preachers, but some of marked originality and power, and also of superior cultivation." Evidently by 1885 we had emerged from the valley and were making our way to the hill-top to take " our place in the sun."

I

A Time of Budding and Foliation.—C. C. M'Kechnie's long term of office as Editor marked an era
in the history of our periodical literature. His
favourite magazine—his own creation—" Springtime," was successfully launched in January 1886,
with a circulation of close upon 20,000. Its taking
title was a parable of the period, reminding us of
Christ's short parable of the Fig-tree : " As soon
as its branches have now become soft and it is
bursting into leaf, you all know that summer is
nigh " (Weymouth's rendering). New buds were
bursting ; larger ideas striving to give themselves
concrete expression. Let us just name some of
these manifestations of vital growth : (1) There are
discernible the small beginnings of army-work
afterwards to attain such remarkable proportions.
(2) The demand for a higher standard of sacred song
for public worship. (3) The growth of social work
and its recognition as a part of Christian service.
(4) A bold advance into a heathendom as yet untouched by the Gospel. (5) Increased provision
for ministerial culture. (6) A more marked and
growing expression of the Christian Democracy
that was implicate in Primitive Methodism. Outstanding representatives of this spirit during the
period were Hugh Gilmore, and Joseph Arch and
John Wilson, both of whom, along with other
Primitive Methodist labour-leaders, were elected
Members of Parliament in 1885.

The New Finance and the Co-ordinating Tendency.—
Nor was this all. " Organisation " and " Consolida-

tion " only lamely describe much that was being done. We cannot fail to perceive that affairs of administration and finance were being dealt with in a new spirit and by methods at once scientific and conscionable—methods conducing to greater efficiency. So, too, with the tendency to co-ordination that was so markedly at work through these years that "THE PERIOD OF CO-ORDINATION" might serve as their fitting label. What was this tendency but the outworking of the growing conviction that all the departments of Church activity were but parts of one whole, had one great end in view, and therefore must be so aligned and related as to be reciprocally helpful.

II. SOME SPECIAL DEVELOPMENTS.

The Small Beginnings of Army Work.—In the report of the General Missionary Committee presented to the Conference of 1885 there is one item which would probably be heard with languid interest when read. As we read it now in the light of the great world-conflagration it gives food for thought. The item reads : " The Committee have also appointed a special agent for work amongst the soldiers at Aldershot, and they have been greatly encouraged by the good results attending this step. They have done a little towards providing a reading-room and library for the soldiers in connection with the mission, and in this good work they will be glad of any sympathy and aid those interested in religious effort amongst the military may be pleased to afford." Evidently it was the day of small things and small expectations in regard to army-work. The quoted reference strikes one as timid, almost apologetic in tone. The truth is, the army was not popular with the bulk of our people. It lay beyond the horizon of their world and the range of their sympathies. There were exceptions we know; but we speak generally. Some of our missionaries undoubtedly did good work in garrison towns and naval stations; but if so, it was mainly on their own initiative. The Mother Church of Methodism from the beginning has taken a wiser line, and has had its reward in so doing.

A New Hymnal for a New Period.—There is no finality in congregational Hymn Books. Their expectation of life seldom extends much beyond the fated thirty years. Each generation of worshippers seems to demand its own Hymnal in order to satisfy its more fastidious taste and meet its growing requirements. Other Churches may have had a different experience; but this has been the experience of our own Church. Of the first Hymn Book, largely based on Lorenzo Dow's, there were many editions issued—some authorised, and still more pirated—from 1809 to 1825, in which latter year the "Large" Hymn Book was published. "Large" implied that the "Small" was not dead or done with. Unchanged, it continued to live on, bound up in the same volume with its bigger companion, until 1853, when both were superseded by

John Flesher's Hymn Book. So it happened that the Small Hymn Book was favoured with a longer life than any other the Connexion has had. It was in 1882—or wanting two years of the thirty—that a committee of fourteen, with Joseph Wood, M.A., as its secretary, was appointed to prepare a new Hymnal. The preface to the volume is dated " November 1886," so that in 1885 the committee had got through the heavier part of its work. In his report to the Conference of 1888 the Book Steward was able to report that in the last few months of the Connexional year no less than 98,760 copies of the Hymnal had been sold.

III.   THE GROWTH AND RECOGNITION OF SOCIAL SERVICE.

The Clapton Mission.—That noble passion we know as "the enthusiasm of humanity" was stirring in the hearts of individuals and groups of individuals at the beginning of this period and took on various forms as the period progressed. Thomas Jackson was one of the delegates sent up to the Reading Conference of 1885, and it behoves us to inquire what were the purposes he cherished just at this time. He found the suggestion and inspiration of his life-work where, and just as, "General" Booth had found his in 1865. On Sunday, October 12th, 1876, when he opened his commission as a home missionary he took his stand in the afternoon on Mile End Waste, and, with no

helpers, sang and preached amid the hubbub, sur-
rounded by blasphemous infidels and boisterous
drunkards. " The experience of that day," says
Mr. Jackson, "greatly distressed me ; but it so
profoundly stirred my soul that I resolved by the
help of God that I would devote myself unreservedly
to the work of serving and saving the poor in the
East End." The vow then registered has been
faithfully kept. The blessing of the hundredfold
has been on his diligent sowing. In this necessarily
brief reference to Thomas Jackson's social and
evangelistic work we begin with the second phase
of that work, and follow its developments from the
winter of 1884 to 1897. Mr. J. S. Parkman, a
generous London layman, having given £100 to
open a new mission, the district of Clapton was
fixed upon. A disused theatre, locally known as
" The Dust-Hole," was acquired and, in July 1884,
Thomas Jackson and his devoted wife began their
labours. At first they two were the only members
of society. In the winter, free breakfasts for the
half-starved children were started, and 10,000
dinners for the poor provided. After twelve
months' work at the Theatre, a society of ninety
members and a Sunday School of 150 scholars and
twelve teachers were reported. In the autumn of
1885 a site was acquired and Clapton Park Tabernacle built. Afterwards the neighbourhood of
Southwold Road was attacked and a mission-hall
erected. Next a temporary Home of Rest at
Southend-on-Sea was opened and a mission started,
with results to be hereafter chronicled.

Official Recognition given to Social Work, 1895.—
It was at this stage that a strong sub-committee
met at Nottingham to consider the whole question
of the relation of Social Work to the missionary
labour of the Church. The date of that important
consultation was January 18th, 1895. It was
resolved : " That we recognise Social Work as a
part of Christian endeavour and service." Then
the conditions to which such work must conform in
order to secure Connexional recognition and financial
help were formulated. Lastly, it was resolved :
" That in our judgment the work carried on by
Mr. Jackson is worthy of the support of our people,
and we authorise the adoption of such means for
its support as Mr. Jackson and the General Missionary Committee may deem desirable." These
are important, far-reaching resolutions ; that is
why they get chronicled and emphasised here.
Yet, remember, they were drafted in 1895, when
the most striking features of Thomas Jackson's
work were still to come. For all that they were
a legitimate development. Thomas Jackson and
they who drafted these resolutions were only making
explicit what was already implicit in the Rules of
1814. They had caught the spirit—humane,
pitiful, brotherly—which breathes through the
whole of the society rules of the first period.

Whitechapel and the Working Lads' Institute.—It
was in October 1896 that, in casually glancing at
" The Christian," Thomas Jackson learned that
the Working Lads' Institute in Whitechapel was

to be sold.   This noble building, that fittingly looks
across to the great London Hospital, had been
opened by Royalty and patronised by philanthropic
city men, yet it had somehow failed to " catch on "
and had fallen on evil days.   The casual reader
put down his paper and stared at a big idea!
" Why, here is an opportunity of a lifetime—one
not to be missed!   Let us buy it for Primitive
Methodism and thus save the noble building from
being perverted to some ignoble use or other ; and
let us make it the centre for vigorous evangelistic
and philanthropic work."   It was a daring and
almost staggering project.   For some time there
was doubt and hesitancy in influential quarters.
But, ultimately, faith in God, and confidence in
Thomas Jackson's judgment and his ability " to
get things done " prevailed.   On December 7th,
1896, the missionary and his wife took possession,
and on April 22nd, 1897, the building was formally
opened.   This is Whitechapel's first phase.   Truly,
a notable twelve years' work!   Starting with the
dilapidated, disreputable " Dust-Hole " and ending
with the acquisition of the—by comparison—
palatial Working Lads' Institute soon to be astir with
its many ameliorative agencies.

The Connexional Orphanage (1889)—as yet
speaking of it as one—is without doubt the most
popular of our institutions.   It was longed for before
it was begun, and since its establishment it has had
a steady course of prosperity—been well officered,
liberally supported, and has grown in favour

with our people. Joseph Peck was the real founder
of the Alresford Orphanage. This plain, unpre-
tentious minister had, or rather was possessed by,
one great idea. A Connexional Orphanage was his
dream by night and the burthen of his prayers by
day. He talked of it with all and sundry; and one
such talk with a lady—Miss Onslow—opened to
him the door of opportunity. Sympathising with
his project, she offered him a suitable building at
a nominal figure—£500—inclusive of furniture, etc.
He closed with the offer and, liberally assisted by
Mr. Walmsley of Leeds, a small trust was formed
and the project brought before the Connexion. The
six Leeds Circuits gave the enterprise a good " send-
off " just on the eve of the Conference of 1889, and
that Conference gave the Orphanage its blessing. Its
first Report was presented in 1890, and in 1897 it
was stated that, since its opening, ninety orphans
had been admitted, and, after training, thirty-five
had left the Home to enter upon situations which
for the most part had been secured by the Committee.

The Southwark Mission.—Like Thomas Jackson,
James Flanagan was a married man and had proved
himself to be an able and very successful mission-
preacher when, in 1891, he received his extraordinary call to the regular ministry and was appointed to the Southwark Mission, which had its
headquarters at Trinity Chapel. By the successive
ministries of some of the Connexion's ablest men
the cause at Trinity had been kept alive; but it
was a rather struggling and disheartened cause.

It had been made clear by this time that the ordinary methods of church-work would not suffice in this poor and densely populated transpontine district. To the missioner and his committee it soon became clear also, that Trinity Chapel neither was, nor could ever be made, a suitable centre for a mission in such a locality. It was a formidable and almost heart-breaking task that James Flanagan had to take up day by day. Yet he and his band of helpers nobly struggled with the difficulties of their position during those years. A live Gospel was preached, and not unsuccessfully; and some novel forms of social service were introduced. Such was the situation when the admirable site on the Old Kent Road was acquired on an eighty years' lease from the Corporation of London. " The Old Kent Tap " must be coupled with " The Old Dust-Hole " of Clapton. Both are symbols. The low drink-shop and the lower—if possible—and more degrading theatre, with their bad record and evil memories, were to be replaced by purifying and saving agencies. And so we leave the Old Kent Tap in course of demolition, and the next period will show us the building of St. George's Hall and the founding of the South-East London Mission.

Aged and Necessitous Local Preachers' Fund.— Few more moving human documents can be met with than the first Report of this Fund which was presented to the Conference of 1897; and the same is true of many of the subsequent Reports. The first one tells how, in the few months the Fund had been in operation, it had helped the necessitous in 134 cases, some of them being over ninety years of age, some blind, some paralysed, and *all* extremely poor. Not a few of the recipients shed tears of joy on receiving the grant, confessing, as they did, that it came in the very nick of time, when they were reduced to the last extremity of want.

IV. A BOLD ADVANCE INTO UNTOUCHED HEATHENDOM.

The South Central African Mission.—A notable missionary advance began when, on April 26th, 1889, a missionary party set sail from Dartmouth. It consisted of H. and Mrs. Buckenham, Arthur Baldwin, and an artisan missionary. Such a departure meant much anxious forethought and elaborate preparation. Well might it be written at the time : " This is the greatest and most important enterprise which our Church has undertaken." It was a bold, adventurous raid into " the clear, open field of untouched heathendom." The missionary party were nearly five years from leaving England before settling down in Mashukulumbwe-land.* The story of their wanderings, hindrances, privations, culminating in the death of Mr. Buckenham on July 11th, 1896, is a veritable missionary Odyssey. The experiences of our heroic pioneers during these trying years have been

* " They arrived in December [1893] and are now engaged in ministering to the people."—*Missionary Report,* 1894.

characterised by the General Missionary Secretary
of the time in unforgettable words :—

" They were often perplexed, weary, worn and sad ;
but, under God, their persistent bravery overcame
all things.   The names of Henry and Mrs. Buckenham and Arthur Baldwin will ever have prominent
places on our Church's roll of fame.   And I doubt not
that in coming years the story of the founding of our
mission in Mashukulumbwe-land will be regarded
as one of the most striking and inspiring examples
of missionary triumph over difficulties in the annals
of missionary enterprise in the nineteenth century."

The demeanour of our people at home during this
long interval of suspense was in every way admirable.
There was no carping, hostile criticism worth the
mention ; no complaining of the lack of quick
returns.   What we see is a self-restraint and calmness born of the conviction that God was in the
enterprise and that in His own good time He would
bring His purposes to pass.   On February 22, 1895,
F. and Mrs. Pickering and W. Chapman had their
God-speed service at Exeter Hall and went out
to reinforce Arthur Baldwin.   In the Missionary
Report for 1897 we are told that two teaching
native evangelists have gone from Aliwal North :
" They are the first-fruits of our educational work
in South Africa, and but the forerunners of a long
line of duly qualified native preachers and teachers
who shall form *an indigenous ministry* which *is the
supreme need of Africa."*   We have italicised the
last words of this excerpt, because they are
eminently characteristic, and express one of the

most settled convictions of the writer—John Smith
—who had the direction of missionary affairs from
1894 to 1899.

The Mission in Southern Nigeria.—Nor was this
the only notable missionary advance made during
this period. Another vast region of the mysterious
Continent was entered and made a veritable "sphere
of influence." It was on December 17, 1893, that
Robert Fairley and J. Marcus Brown held their
first service at *Archibongville* in the Old Palaver
House. (Let the coincidence be noted that this
event occurred only four days before Messrs. Buckenham and Baldwin had reached the end of their
toilsome journeyings). It was the high-handed
procedure of the Spanish governor in closing our
schools in Fernando Po that led to the founding of
this mission in Southern Nigeria. To this cross-
providence we owe "our brightest missionary
page." The necessity of providing a sure base
and all needful educational facilities for our West
African work was the motive that induced the
authorities to take quick action and execute a
purpose which had been thought of, it seems, as far
back as 1870. Hence after due enquiries and
preparations had been made on the spot, the
territory of Prince Archibong was fixed upon, and
the beginning made to which we have referred.
We still retain Archibongville, but some years
ago a more healthy location was acquired at ORON
in British territory. James Travis was General
Missionary Secretary when this fruitful mission had

its inception, and it will be well to have his mature
judgment on its value put on record :—

"I do not know of anything in the modern history of
African Missions more enchanting and inspiring than
the story of our Missions in Southern Nigeria during the
last twenty years. As I think of the extent to which our
dreams of the early 'nineties have been realised and of the
signs and wonders which God has wrought through our
Church in this district in the course of these few years,
my heart swells with grateful and joyous amazement.
Surely the age of miracles is still with us ! " *

V.   THE HIGHER FINANCE AND ADMINISTRATIVE
REFORM.

"This also cometh forth from Jehovah of hosts, who is
wonderful in counsel, and excellent in that sort of wisdom which
causes things to succeed."
ISA. XXVIII. 29 (Dr. George Adam Smith's rendering).

The Chapel Aid Association.—It must be patent
to any one who considers the matter closely that
during this period church affairs on their material
side were being attended to after a new and improved fashion.   Had our leaders insensibly caught
and appropriated something of the prevailing
scientific spirit of their time, but blending it har-
moniously with the essential Christian spirit, which
views all things—£ s. d., bricks and mortar, and
Church-machinery of every kind—in Him, and
therefore to be-held as secondary, and carefully
used in His service ?   It would almost seem so.
If we fall back on the phrase " the consecration of

* See James Travis' illuminative book : " Seventy-Five
Years," pp. 124-5.

business faculty in the service of the Church," then
the thing so designated was markedly in evidence
from 1885 onward. Let one or two conspicuous
examples of its working be glanced at. The
establishment of such an institution as the Chapel
Aid Association would give distinction to any
period. It has been called, and rightly, " a triumph
of financial genius," and we owe its inception to
Mr. W. P. Hartley. There can be no doubt that
his entry into Connexional affairs at this juncture
was an untold blessing, not merely because of the
perennial flow of his benefactions, but because
he placed his financial skill unstintedly at the
service of his Church. He has set himself the task
of creating new institutions—like the Chapel Aid
and Church Extension Fund—informed with the
spirit of efficiency, and in assisting to put new life
and vigour into old institutions like the Book Room
and the Missionary Society. In all his giving—
and he has given in a princely way—he has ever
kept in view the desirability of safeguarding the
spirit of self-help, and by example and precept
enforcing the principle of systematic and propor-
tionate giving for worthy causes. Thus much we
cannot forbear saying, once for all ; and this seems
to be the time for saying it. Mr. W. P. Hartley
was ably seconded by a group of men of affairs and
financial skill in the launching of the Chapel Aid
Association—men like John Atkinson, Thomas
Mitchell, James Travis, W. Beckworth, John
Coward and W. R. Bootland. The proposed
scheme was closely scanned. Some doubted :

Hugh Gilmore, however, never did doubt for a moment. It bore the closest scrutiny, and it triumphed. The Chapel Aid Association received the endorsement of Conference as early as 1886, but the work of floating a Company is necessarily a slow process. Its modest first Report was presented in 1890, and by 1897 its Secretary, John Atkinson, was able to state that, during the seven years the Company had been in active operation, trustees had been able to reduce their liabilities £36,196.

The Reconstitution of the Missionary Society.—Our readers will remember what was said of the radical Liverpool legislation conceived in a time of Connexional anxiety. That legislation was not dead all this time, but through much discussion and some criticism, was on its merits winning its way to acceptance. This it got at the long last, at the Conference of 1888. Well may the real author of this legislation, in commenting on this tardy fruition of his hopes and endeavours, write : " So slow and well-considered were the steps taken."

In 1895 the BOOK COMMITTEE was reconstituted. All through the 'fifties it had been a small special one composed of persons resident in or near the metropolis. For the three years ending in 1850 it consisted of but three persons. For a few years after this it was a mixed committee of ministers and laymen, never exceeding ten in number. Then in 1863 the Book Committee lost its separateness and was but the General Committee discharging special functions under the direction of the General

Book Steward.   At the close of our period, however, a body was assigned it and it became an efficient Committee *ad hoc*.   Thus the General Committee, with no shrinkage of numbers, was left free to attend to its own special business.

VI.   THE CO-ORDINATING CONFERENCE OF 1892.

" We must think of a unity, the parts of which are what they are, only in relation to one another and to the whole.   It is not allowable to take one in abstraction from another, or to think of it as independent."

DR. JAMES IVERACH.

The Thanksgiving Fund.—Among the memorable Conferences in our history that of Norwich in 1892 must deservedly take high rank.   It not only endorsed and registered; it created.   Missionary affairs bulked largely at this Conference, so that it was fitting that the General Missionary Secretary, James Travis, should be its President, with Mr. W. P. Hartley, the Treasurer, its Vice-President.   As 1893 was the Jubilee Year of the Missionary Society, it was proposed to celebrate the event by raising £5,000 for the funds of the Society.   But, by a happy inspiration of the Vice-President, a much more ambitious scheme was outlined.   It was now suggested that the sum to be aimed at by the Thanksgiving Fund should be ten times more than the £5,000 first thought of, and that its beneficiary scope should be so enlarged as to include four of the most necessitous funds, namely—the College Ex-

K

tension, the contemplated General Chapel Fund (for which T. Mitchell had already raised £3,000 since 1890), the Superannuated Ministers' Widows' and Orphans', and the Missionary Jubilee. These proposals were adopted amid a scene of great enthusiasm. The President and Vice-President, together with Thomas Mitchell, earned for themselves the title " The Three Jubilee Campaigners." They did not spare themselves during those years in travelling and speaking in the interests of the Thanksgiving Fund. It owed much to their advocacy in various centres of Connexional life; and although the amount aimed at was not raised by 1897, as had been suggested, it *was* raised in the end, and, by skilful finance, all of it was made available for needy Connexional objects. One thing—one might almost say *the* thing—that makes this Norwich Conference so memorable is, the vidence it affords that those who had the direction of affairs were thinking things together, and so they tried to put them together for the sake of the one great object they had, in common.

Manchester College Affairs at the Co-ordinating Conference.—We must remember that Professor A. S. Peake, M.A.'s appointment as Tutor to Manchester College, and the lengthening of the term of residence to two years, both date from the Conference of 1892. In 1891 Mr. W. P. Hartley had offered the Conference £500 per annum for five years, on condition that the students' term of residence should be extended and the services of a University graduate secured. The Norwich Conference gave its hearty endorsement to these suggestions. Dr. Peake (as yet Arthur S. Peake, M.A.) and Principal Fairbairn of Mansfield College were both present during the sittings of Conference and gave addresses at the great meeting on College affairs. We may, perhaps, recapture something of the deep impression their words made at the time if we try to visualise the scene if but for a flash-light moment. Dr. Potts, the representative of the great Methodist Church of Canada, is sitting by the side of the President. We see him leaning over to the President as he whispers in his ear : " That young man is a great gift to your Church ! " It was a true prophecy—destined to be progressively and abundantly fulfilled. Then began an influence which was to do so much to create the desire not only for an alliance, but for a synthesis, between Culture and Evangelism. The beautiful stained-glass window which was unveiled by Mr. W. P. Hartley at the great historic Missionary ·Jubilee meeting in Wesley's Chapel in May 1893 was a symbol. That window was one of a series of presentations from the daughter Churches of Methodism to the Mother Church. The history, the aims, the genius of Primitive Methodism are symbolised by that window. Evangelism—whether at home or abroad—is ever the chief thing. On it all lines should converge ; with it all forms of Church activity be closely co-ordinated.

VII.   DEVELOPMENT OF INSTITUTIONS.

The First Extension of Manchester College.—It was at the Edinburgh Conference of 1895 that Mr. W. P. Hartley showed his unflagging interest in College affairs by generously offering to make provision for the accommodation of sixty students. This was done between 1895 and 1897. A new wing was built parallel with the original building, while the front was extended by the addition of entrance-hall, new dining-hall, library and lecture-hall. The extension was made at a cost of some £12,000, the whole of which Mr. Hartley defrayed. "The opening ceremony," we are told, "was in every respect worthy of the occasion, and the public meeting at night in the Free Trade Hall was perhaps the most largely attended and enthusiastic meeting ever held in the city of Manchester in connection with Primitive Methodism. The address of Dr. Fairbairn, Principal of Mansfield College, was a most suitable, inspiring and helpful utterance." The finishing touches to the extension were given after its formal opening by the erection of the clock-tower. The clock had this peculiarity : human forethought had so predetermined its movements that all day long it chimed the hours and quarters, but kept silent from 10 p.m. to 7 a.m. !

The Book Room Removed to Aldersgate.—For fifty-two years the Book Room had been located at Sutton Street, Commercial Road, E., but now another migration was necessary. The property was held on lease from the Mercers' Company, and the lease would expire in 1897. Negotiations were entered upon with the lessors, but, as the conditions proved unacceptable, fresh quarters had to be sought. Quite apart from the impending expiry of the lease there were cogent reasons for a change. The lapse of half a century had made Sutton Street much less suitable for a denominational centre than it was when the Editor and Missionary Secretary both lived within the gated enclosure adjoining the chapel and Book Room premises. At that time there was a certain fitness in such a location. The east and north-east of London had long been a stronghold of Nonconformity. But that day was past. Even our own Connexional Committees by this time had flitted from Sutton Street to New Surrey Chapel—a name redolent of Nonconformist traditions. So it is not surprising that the sites-committee should have turned its attention to the centre of London's book-trade. A goodly block of buildings at the junction of Jewin and Aldersgate Streets, the property of the Hon. Goldsmiths' Company, was acquired for the term of sixty-five years for the sum of £7,850. The necessary structural alterations were at once proceeded with and costly electric plant and heating apparatus installed. On June 6th, 1895, the new Book Depôt was opened in the presence of a large and representative gathering. The cover of our chief denominational magazine—"The Aldersgate"—is a periodic souvenir of our sixteen years' occupancy of the Aldersgate Street premises

CHAPTER IX.

The Church Period and the Centenary Years.

" A form of Church extension as urgent as any other is the extension inwards on us of the Church idea and practice."
PRINCIPAL FORSYTH, D.D.

I. FROM " CONNEXION " TO " CHURCH."

The Claim to be a Church Made.—We have not to look long or searchingly to find the distinctive " note " of this period. By this time the consciousness of Church-life had quickened within the erstwhile " Connexion " ; and it is the outworking of this consciousness which explains a good deal we meet with as we go forward to the Centenary years. We are officially designated a " Church " on the class-tickets of 1902 ; and in the " Consolidated Minutes " of the same year, " Church " is substituted for " Connexion " whenever it can be done. But Conferential enactment and official usage usually follow rather than precede the prevailing sentiment of our people. The Conference often signs and seals what has gradually come to be " most surely believed among us," or tested by practice. So the awareness that we had attained to true Church-life nowhere finds clearer declaration than in the " Address to the

Churches " of 1898. In that address such explicit claims are made as " Our credentials as a Church are before the world," " Our Connexion is a great Church."

Conference prepares for and adjusts itself to the Claim. —For some years before 1898 there are signs that the Conference was becoming alive to the fact that it was something more than a big business committee acting in the interests of a number of federated districts. It was getting " to know what belonged to itself " in the way of orderliness, dignity and decorum. We have already written of the evolution of the chairman of a day into the President of the entire sessions of Conference and on through our ecclesiastical year. A further evolutionary step was taken in 1886 by the appointment of Henry Hodge to the Vice-Presidency. He was the first of a long line of eminent laymen who have filled that position. Then, in 1889, came the elaborate legislation in answer to the question, " What shall be done in order to improve the present Order of Procedure in conducting Conference business ? " Another enactment that in practice has made for quicker despatch of business and greater effectiveness was the appointment of a Stationing Committee. Then, too, the old time-wasting, promiscuous method of nominating and electing the chief Connexional officers has gone for ever. Other regulations and usages have gradually come into force, all tending to give fuller recognition and added prestige to the chief officers of the Conference,

and especially to ensure their presence at the
Conference next ensuing. The " Minutes of Conference " have since 1916 become " The Primitive
Methodist Year Book." The "Address to the
Churches " is now "A Pastoral." It is no longer
anonymous, but prepared by the Ex-President,
takes precedence of the rest of the contents of the
Year Book, and is to be read by authority to all the
churches. " These are but small matters," it may
be said. They are, if taken singly ; but if taken
in combination, as they should be, they give sure
indications of the trend of things. The trend is un-
mistakable ; it is in the direction of the orderly
and becoming, and can be observed with no misgivings.

II. The Church in some of•its External Relations.

The Education Committee " appointed to watch the
interests of our Church as they are affected by the
different phases of the Education question " presented
its first report in 1898. It was not a report of work
done, so much as it was an able manifesto of our Connexional policy in regard to this vexed and complex
question. The Conference adopted the report and
affirmed that the policy outlined in the manifesto
was to be taken as the programme of our Church.
From this time the report of the Education Committee, long signed by James Pickett, its Secretary

becomes a regular feature of the Minutes of Conference. No denomination was more vitally affected by the Government legislation than our own, because of the heavy stake we hold in the villages. During the formative period of the Sunday School Union many glaring cases of clerical intolerance, pivoting on the parish day-school and loudly crying for a remedy, were brought to light. Further evidence pointing the same moral was furnished by the valuable report on " Towns and Villages " which was presented in 1896. A book should be written recounting the course of the long struggle and the part our Church has taken in it in the way both of doing and suffering. Here it is enough to say that much Connexional energy has been thrown into this conflict on behalf of religious liberty. The reactionary Education Act of 1902 roused strong opposition. The newly-formed London Primitive Methodist Council was especially active in its opposition to the objectionable features of the Act ; while during his Presidency of the National Council of the Evangelical Free Churches Mr. Travis threw himself with characteristic ardour into the struggle, and did excellent service by his rousing, fighting speeches. It has been stated on good authority that the first passive-resister was a Wirksworth Circuit Primitive Methodist. His example was followed by many throughout the country. Imprisonment was the lot of some, while a still greater number joyfully suffered " the spoiling of their goods " rather than pay the obnoxious tax.

Our Relations with the National Council of the Evangelical Free Churches have from the beginning been close and sympathetic. Some of the leaders of our Church took a prominent part in its formation. Thomas Mitchell, an expert in finance and to the finger-tips a man of affairs, was the second Primitive Methodist to be elected to the Presidency of the Council. This honour came to him and the Church he served so well in 1912. The once famous Free Church Catechism, which Hugh Price Hughes sanguinely believed would, in the course of twenty years, come to be regarded as " one of the most wonderful and far-reaching facts of the wonderful century now hasting to its close,"* was issued in 1898. Professor A. S. Peake, D.D., and H. B. Kendall, B.A., were our representatives on the Committee which prepared it. Many of our ministers and College students took an active part in the great Simultaneous Mission which ushered in the Twentieth Century. J. Tolefree Parr, of Surrey Chapel, was lent to the National Council that he might be its ministerial Missioner, 1901–9. A. T. Guttery, our President of the London Conference of 1916, is the National Council's designated President for 1919. Lastly, with gratification we note multiplying signs of the growing friendliness between our Church and the Mother Church of Methodism. In these days the comity of the Churches is showing itself in many ways ; in none more interesting than in the beginnings of co-operation between City Road and Holborn Hall in Book Trade matters.

* *Contemporary Review*, Jan. 1899.

Negotiations for Union with the Bible Christians.—
Brief reference must here be made to these protracted negotiations which began in 1894 and
extended to 1900. " Of all words of tongue and
pen, the saddest are ' it might have been ' " ; and this
is one of the might-have-beens of our history. Little
profit in dwelling on what never came off ! Enough
to say, the question was finally disposed of by the
referendum which was taken throughout the Connexion between the Conferences of 1899–1900.
The Conference gave judgment accordingly : " That
it is not desirable to continue negotiations for organic
union at present." It may seem a pity for such
high hopes to have been kindled and fanned only
to be quenched ; for six years' well-intentioned
labour to go for nothing. But the ideal was only
postponed and not banished for ever. We shall
see it again by-and-by ; and we shall see it in a
more alluring form.

III. SOME FRESH UNFOLDINGS OF CHURCH LIFE.

*The Sustentation Fund, 1898, and Church Extension
Fund, 1900.*—" The adoption of legislation con-
stituting the General Fund into a General Missionary and Sustentation Fund marks a new departure."
The act thus officially described came at once into
operation. It was a just and honest measure. It
put an end to some anomalies and encouraged
many a hard-working home-missionary. The
starting of this Fund was at first the creation of a

new missionary department. By this time one
might have thought the title of the Committee was
quite long enough. But no; it soon became
necessary to lengthen it still further in order to a
completer definition. In 1900 its style and title
became the " General Missionary, Sustentation and
Church Extension Fund Committee." The essential
thing to notice here is that, despite the ambiguity
that may seem to lurk in its name, the Church
Extension Fund is a thoroughly *missionary* department. It was missionary in its demand and inception, and it is missionary still, through and
through, in its aim and workings.

It is not churches " made with hands " that
bound its vision, but the establishment of living
Churches where they are most needed—in London
and its suburbs, in rapidly rising localities, in coast
and inland watering-places. This was the purport
of the legislation as laid before the Bristol Conference of 1900 which, in no perfunctory fashion,
made it law. It was Mr. W. P. Hartley who in
Committee had given the formulated scheme the
final touch which made all the difference ; and it
was he who, in its final shape, read the scheme to
the assembled delegates who received it with acclaim.
Under the administration of Thomas Mitchell, who
continued in office nine years, the success of the
Church Extension Fund was amply demonstrated.
In 1912 it was reported that " no less than 240
churches and Sunday Schools owe their initiation
to the fact that the Church Extension Fund has been
able to promise interest for a term of years on part

of the cost. These new erections have cost over
£400,000. With the movement of population into
suburbs, and the rapid growth of towns and cities,
thousands of our members *would be lost to the Church*
if buildings were not erected in these new neigh-
bourhoods." The Church Extension Fund is
an eminently conservative as well as aggressive
organisation, as is indicated by the words we have
put in italics. T. Mitchell was succeeded in the
secretariat by H. J. Taylor, and he in turn, under
the new five years' rule, by John Mayles, the present
Financial Secretary. Not only did the General
Missionary Committee thus trifurcate itself; it
put forth, so to speak, friendly tentacles, and made
attachments with other Connexional organisations
—in this way. As the Chapel Aid, the Insurance
Company, and the General Chapel Fund were all
more or less concerned and co-operant in the working
of the Church Extension Fund, care was taken to
have representatives of these bodies on the board
of the Missions Quarterly Committee. Representation was also given to the Ladies' Missionary
Association, the S.S. Union on its missionary side,
and the Laymen's League. The idea here, evidently
striving to express and organically articulate itself,
is that the Church is essentially a missionary
organisation, and that all its parts and connexions
must be made contributory to sending out the
light and truth of the Gospel. This conception,
with its associated interlinking policy, has had its
abundant reward in quickened missionary enthusiasm and all that follows in its train—willing-

hearted labourers in plenty, augmented missionary income, and phenomenal success on the foreign field. These are amongst the brightest—indeed they are the redeeming—features of recent years.

General Sunday School Union Developments.— You observe precisely the same dove-tailing and " togethering " process at work in the General Sunday School Union as in the missionary depart- ment during this period. This creates a difficulty for any one who has a fondness for keeping things logically clear and distinct. But when one sees why it is so the difficulty is almost welcomed. Life can, and does, combine what Logic persists in keep- ing asunder. So with the truly alive Sunday School Union. The single word " Education " will cover many of its activities, but not all by any means ; not " cradle-roll " or Holiday Tours, for example. The fact is we wake up to realise that there has somehow come into existence a Church within the Church—the " Church of the worshipping children " —a complex Church, as varied in its interests as the adult Church of which it is the counterpart. For this discovery we ought to have been prepared. Right down through the years we have—perhaps rather absent-mindedly—been used to call the Sunday School the " nursery of the Church." We may have thought of the domestic nursery, but is it not the nursery of the horticulturist that is meant ? The very word should have prepared us for what we are now seeing ; for the slips and seedlings of the nursery are of the same kind as the flowers and trees of the garden and shrubbery, though for the time being they may grow in a separate enclosure and require different treatment. A new conception of the Sunday School and of its possibilities is evidently winning its way in these latter days. The anxious solicitude of each successive Conference for the success of the institution—even the Conference's occasional fallings into microscopic investigation and fault-findings—grow out of the conviction that, as things are, the success or failure of her Sunday Schools is a vital matter—vital, because to them she must mainly look for her replenishment and perpetuation. "The nearest way to the Millennium is through the Sunday Schools."*

Christian Endeavour and Temperance and Band of Hope.—The Young People's Society of Christian Endeavour had already taken root in the Connexion when in 1896 the legislation was placed upon the statute book that was to govern its operations. The growth of this movement as well as of Temperance made it expedient that these two sections should become separate departments. This was done in 1898 when G. Bennett was named Christian Endeavour Secretary and T. H. Hunt Temperance Secretary. These were admirable appointments and augured well for the success of both movements. In 1899 the rules governing the Society of Christian Endeavour were revised in order to bring them more into harmony with the

* S. Horton in the Address to the Churches, 1908.

identical purpose of the National Union of Christian Endeavour. At this time, too, with the aid of the General Missionary Committee, Miss Perrett had begun her fruitful labours as Sunday School Evangelist. The Endeavour movement took increasing hold of the young life of the Church. Its influence for good has been felt in many directions, and its activities have taken some interesting developments—literary, recreative and missionary. *Springtime* was adapted to be the organ of the Society. A READING UNION was begun of which P. McPhail was made the director. Under his guidance the Reading Union still prospers. The Endeavour has also its HOLIDAY TOUR DEPARTMENT which has widened its range and become increasingly popular. In 1905, as the result of an appeal, the Societies throughout the Connexion raised nearly £1,000 to defray the cost of the Oron Training Institute for the equipment of native teachers. Nor was this all; they pledged themselves to its maintenance and have nobly redeemed their pledge.

It should be recalled that in 1889 the *Bible Reading and Prayer Union* was launched. From the evidence brought forward by Mr. S. S. Henshaw there can be little doubt that to Mr. J. W. Hives rightly belongs the honour of being the founder of this department, and he was its Secretary until his lamented death in 1898.

Among the later developments of the S.S. Union have been the Anti-Cigarette League (1905), the formation of the Young People's Missionary Department (1906), and the Cradle Roll (1907). The Morse Lecture was founded in 1905, and the first lecture under that foundation was given at the Triennial Conference of 1907 by T. H. Hunt— *Sunday School Reform : a Problem for the Times ;* the second in 1910 by S. S. Henshaw—*The Romance of our Sunday Schools.* The S.S. Union has come under, and responded to, the scientific spirit of the time. It has sought to promote the grading of its schools into the three departments — primary, intermediate and senior. It has improved its methods of teaching, made its annual competitive examinations for both teachers and scholars at once more efficient and popular. What is more, it has instituted a well-thought-out scheme of teacher-training which embraces Bible-knowledge, child study and teaching methods.

IV.   FURTHER DEVELOPMENT OF INSTITUTIONS.

The Working Lads' Institute.—At the close of the last period we left Thomas Jackson and the society he directed located in this noble building in London's broadest thoroughfare. For three years he pursued his varied evangelical and social agencies—and then the unforeseen happened. The rear part of the building was required for railway extension, and the sum of £20,000 had to be paid over for the compulsory sale of the part required. Besides the sale price, all damage caused to the part still retained was to be made good. The debt

L

of £9,200 was paid off and all money borrowed from the Missionary Committee returned. In 1894 a temporary Home of Rest had been opened at Southend. As the outcome of this extension Southend was formed into a station including Southend, Shoeburyness, Southchurch, and Leigh-on-Sea. In 1902 the present Home of Rest was opened at a cost of £3,800. It is now debtless, and the property at Whitechapel and Southend in 1905 was valued at £30,000. One may see a great propriety in the fact that the brave home missionary and friend of the destitute and friendless was, with the good wishes of his brethren, made President of the Conference of 1912. But though we may make 1912 the end of our period it was not to be the end of Mr. Jackson's work. In 1914 the Missionary Report announces that the trustees of the late Benjamin Walmsley of Leeds offered to the Connexion the Orphanage, Church and Sunday Schools at Brudenell Road, Leeds, established by Mr. Walmsley. After consultation with the Leeds friends it was determined to open a Home for destitute lads and first offenders, and for the time being to make it a Branch of Whitechapel. The suggestion was acted upon. Accordingly on the stations for that year we have: " Leeds: Brudenell Road Mission Branch, John Moseley, Lay Evangelist (under care of Thomas Jackson)."

The South-East London Mission.—At the opening of this period, " the better workshop " James Flanagan had desired was being supplied. The

" Old Kent Tap " was soon no more seen and the walls of St. George's Hall gradually reared themselves skyward. On January 4th, 1900, the dedicatory sermon of the new building was preached by Hugh Price Hughes, M.A. By the opening day Mr. Flanagan's exertions had resulted in the raising of £8,000, so that there remained but £1,000 of debt on the property. In a month this was liquidated, leaving only the debt on the organ and fixtures.

The establishment of a SISTERS' SETTLEMENT and Training Home was another of James Flanagan's big ideas. This materialised in 1901 and, as the 17th Report—1918—shows, the work of the Sisters has proved an untold blessing to this crowded district and, we may add, the Settlement's influence for good has been felt far beyond the Thames. In 1902 Joseph Johnson was " translated " from Stoke Newington, after fourteen years of remarkable success, to become the superintendent of the Mission and to carry on and still further develop the work. In 1905 the Cripples' Seaside Home—now located at Westcliff-on-Sea, and the only Home of its kind in British Methodism—was founded by Joseph Johnson. Meanwhile James Flanagan had set himself to the herculean task of raising the money required for purchasing the freehold of the property. By 1905 it was done: the £3,500 had been raised. In accomplishing this feat Mr. Flanagan gave proof of unsuspected powers. Every one knew he was a man of uncommon mould—eloquent, with more than a touch of genius and poetic faculty in his composition ; but this campaign showed that, behind all this, there burned a steady fire of altruistic passion, and a will set and strong enough to turn visions into facts.   In 1915, after 13 years' strenuous and most successful work at St. George's Hall, Joseph Johnson became General Book Steward, and was succeeded by H. J. Taylor. Under his capable direction the old ministries have gone forward and new developments are taking form and substance. Nor is this the whole account of what was being done throughout this period in the way of Christian Social Service. It must stand as a type and sample. We must remember the continuous work pursued at Clapton Mission, and at Surrey Chapel, Blackfriars, and Livingstone Hall, Edinburgh—acquired in 1902. By all means let our readers procure the volume which tells of the devoted labours of Sister Annie in Blackfriars,* and not fail to read the report of what is being done year by year at our other mission centres such as "Bethel," Sheffield, and "Rehoboth," Leeds.

Hartley College, Second Extension.—It might almost have seemed that finality had been reached when, in 1898, the clock-tower was reared and the library built and furnished. But no ; another unforeseen reach opened out and progress was resumed. "Our unfailing benefactor" gave renewed proof of the statement that "a ministry at once cultured and evangelical is his ideal." Many who sat in the Central Church, Newcastle-on-Tyne, in

* By J. Tolefree Parr, President of 1917.

1903, got the surprise of their lives when, in a quiet tone and as though he were asking instead of conferring a favour, Sir William—as we will anticipatively call him—offered to enlarge the College so as to provide for the accommodation of forty additional students. Sir William supplemented his first offer by proposing to build a College Chapel and library. This second Extension was inaugurated at the Conference of 1906. John G. Bowran in the Conference Address notes that Hartley " is the largest denominational College in the land and that the ceremony of the opening was one of the most brilliant scenes in all our history." Dr. Fairbairn preached the first sermon in the College Chapel and Dr. J. Hope Moulton gave an address at the great gathering in the Free Trade Hall. In 1912, the end of our period, Professor Peake was just entering on his twenty-first year of high service at the College. It was resolved suitably to commemorate the event. To keep like things together, we may note how this was done in 1913. A subscription portrait of Prof. Peake was unveiled by Sir William ; and in the Minutes of 1914 the latter is thanked for his munificent gifts on this commemorative occasion —for three stained-glass windows designed by Mr. R. Anning Bell, A.R.A., placed in the transept and chancel of the College, also for the endowment of twelve scholarships at Hartley College tenable during the first and second years' residence, and for adding to the Whitehead scholarship so as to make it adequate for the fees of the College for one year.

V. Table of Other Notabilia of the Period
1898–1912.

Other Happenings and Developments of these busy, crowded years must, for the sake of brevity, be compressed and presented in tabular form. The table may conduce to clearness and be useful for reference.

1898 The Second Hartley Lecture (though the first published) given by Dr. J. Watson. The Lectureship was founded by Sir W. P. Hartley and the first was given by Dr. J. Ferguson in 1897.

,,   The Candidates' Oral Examining Committee begins.

1899 The first lady representative takes her seat in Conference.

,,   Joseph Odell receives the thanks of Conference for his work in Birmingham and for the success which has attended his direction of the Evangelists' Home founded in 1886.

,,   Silver Jubilee of the General Sunday School Union attained.

1900 The South Australian Churches with 3,167 members unite with the Methodist Church of Australia.

1901 Superannuated ministers become eligible for election on the Deed Poll.

1902 Representation of Districts to Conference is put on a numerical basis.

,,   Fortnightly Missionary Committee abolished.

1903 Harrogate is fixed upon as the location of the new Orphan Homes. In 1912 there were 53 orphans at Alresford and 48 in the Harrogate Homes.

1904 Elaborate legislation to be put in force for the Training and Examination of local preachers.

1905 The Connexional increase for the year is 4,638, the largest since 1833.

,,   The Evangelists' Home discontinued, and J. Odell and J. Flanagan set apart as Connexional Evangelists.

,,   Sir W. P. Hartley gives £3,000 for the reduction of debt on London chapels.

1906 The office of Financial Secretary made separate and distinct.

1907 Wonderful resurrection of Elmfield : henceforward to be under the management of the " old boys."

1908 Primitive Methodist Social Service Union recognised and blessed by Conference.

1909 Oron Training Institute has sent out nine native evangelists.

1910 *Hymnal Supplement* Committee appointed.

1911 President of Conference to be designated a year in advance.

1912 Last appearance of New Zealand on the stations, as it elects to join the Methodist Church of Australasia.

,,   The *Hymnal Supplement* completed. Preface dated January 1912.

1912   More Connexional offices brought under the
five years' limitation.

,,   African Missionary revenue for the first time
reaches £10,000.

,,   "The six Mission Vans have had a successful
year." The first began in 1893.

,,   The Primitive Methodist Insurance Company
has given £30,000 to Connexional objects
since its formation in 1864.

,,   Last echo of the Centenary : the closing of
the accounts.

,,   Holborn Hall transferred to the Connexion
on December 31st.

VI. An Abiding Centenary Memorial.

Holborn Hall, Gray's Inn Road, London, that now
becomes the Connexional Headquarters, was built
in 1875 and acquired from the Holborn Borough
Authorities in the year 1908 by Sir William P.
Hartley, with a view to its becoming the Connexional
centre. It was held by him until 1912 when, at
the request of the Conference, it was conveyed to
the Bourne Trust Corporation, Limited, to be held
in trust for the denomination, for the sum of
£56,700. Meanwhile, two additional floors with a
suite of commodious offices had been added to the
premises, whilst at the rear, on the Clerkenwell
side of the building, there had been erected a five-
floor block for the requirements of the Publishing
House. The transference of the Book Room from

Aldersgate Street to the Connexion's new head-quarters at Holborn Hall was effected in 1910. This involved an immense amount of thought and ingenuity on the part of the Book Steward of that period—Edwin Dalton, D.D. In succeeding him, William A. Hammond had the responsibility of letting the offices, and in setting the pace for the general administration of the premises. A grant of £7,500 was made from the Centenary Fund and supplemented by a gift of a similar amount from Sir William P. Hartley, so that the Connexion acquired the possession and control of these magnificent premises, valued at £65,000, for less than £42,500. At the Nottingham Conference of 1916, Sir William, as a Golden Wedding Thanks-giving, made a further gift to these premises of £10,000, payable in four yearly instalments. The Connexion has here a valuable set of premises suitable to its requirements as its official head-quarters, and likely to prove a remunerative asset from a business point of view. The acquisition of Holborn Hall would of itself make 1912 a red-letter year in our Connexional annals. It is a solid way-mark of our Church progress. At last we had got an enclave in the metropolis—our own Church House. Holborn Hall is, indeed, likely to prove the most striking and tangible monument of our Centenary and of the foresight and princely generosity of Sir William Hartley. These thoughts naturally lead on to a brief survey of the course and results of the Centenary celebrations,

VII. The Centenary Years.

"Happily for us, ... the Primitive Methodist Society has enriched the annals of grace in its hundred years of life more than any three centuries of mediæval life in England."

"Mow Cop, one of the holy places of the earth, where Primitive Methodism secured its first initial baptism, and where, if it please God, it may again, in the course of the Centenary year, be baptised for the dead."

Dr. Rendel Harris.

Some Tangible Results of the Centenary.—Though the fleeting, transitory element belonged to the Centenary, as it did to the Queen's Diamond Jubilee, the Centenary did leave some very tangible results. By the spirit of liberality it evoked throughout the Connexion, the depleted coffers of many worthy institutions were replenished, and this monetary relief contributed to their easier and more efficient working. In the final balance sheet of the Centenary Fund presented in 1912, we have there set out the Funds that participated in the benefit, and to what extent, and we cannot but note with satisfaction that almost every Fund figures in the list. There had been other Thanksgiving Funds in the history of our Church, but never one so successfully organised or so lucrative as this. Besides these general Connexional interests that were permanently eased and benefited, there was the preponderating sum that was raised for local purposes. The sum aimed at was £250,000—two-fifths to go to Connexional objects, and three-fifths to local purposes. In the latter case this proportion was exceeded, while the sum raised for Connexional purposes came short of the contemplated £100,000.

In the aggregate, however, the results exceeded the sum aimed at by over £77,000.   Then, too, we have to take into account the permanent literary out-come of the Centenary, which was considerable. Here it would be a pleasure to linger and to particularise.   But it cannot be done ; and it were a folly to attempt it, for it has already been done as well as could be by J. Day Thompson's really brilliant book, *The Church that Found Herself*.   Mr. Thompson's must always be the standard History of the Centenary, and to it the reader is referred for the details of the movement from its foreshadowing in 1903 to its consummation.   Our business will not be to describe, but merely to note and comment on one or two salient points of the celebration.

A Triumph of Organisation.—The Centenary from start to finish was splendidly organised.   The Conference appointed a Committee of fifty to lay the first planks and start the movement.   The right note was struck at the first meeting of this constitutive committee.   A high ideal, to be kept in view throughout the celebration, was clearly and even eloquently stated by Editor, Henry Yooll, subscribed by the Committee, and ratified by the Conference.   The Grand Committee, now aug-mented to one hundred by representatives from the Districts, proceeded to divide itself into three sections, evangelistic, literary and financial.   It is when we come to the decision that gifts for local purposes should reckon as part of the £250,000 aimed at, that doubt arises whether this was not

a concession to the sectional tendencies that were
yet far from dead. " The ideal," critics might
say, " would have been to concentrate on one fund
for general Connexional purposes." The result of
the decision taken gives some point to the criticism.
The appointments of John Welford and George
Armstrong to be the General and Organising secretaries were happy and far-sighted ones. How often
we read that every crisis or great world-movement
" throws up " some strong man to control or guide it !
It is a shabby phrase, smacking of atheism. Not so
do the Scriptures speak of the advent of men for
their times. " There was a man sent from God
whose name was John." The secretaries were
ably supported by the Connexional leaders from
the Presidents downwards. So, we repeat the
celebration was a triumph of organisation, and the
course and outcome of it deeply underscore what
has already been said of the higher and more conscionable dealing with matters of organisation and
finance that forms so marked a feature of the latest
periods.

An Object-lesson to the Churches and the Public.—
The Centenary gatherings on Mow Cop in 1907 and
1910 smote the public eye and made a decided
impression. The *Daily Mail's* staring headline,
" Sixty Thousand Methodists on a Mountain ! "
bore witness to that. Reporters—that curious
class, detached, quizzical, and always on the look-out
for the queer and the abnormal—posted to our
" Mount of memories." But they did not mock,

They were, it would seem, a little puzzled and at fault.   They noted, with a touch of surprise, the absence of the spectacular ; they had almost expected a drum and trumpet demonstration.   To speak truly, they were a little moved by the old hymns and by the simplicity and sincerity of the whole proceedings.   The wonder seemed to lie in the bright faces, the camaraderie, the exuberant feeling never verging on extravagance, only showing itself in song ᵥand pious ejaculation, the readiness to speak and the eagerness to listen.   The presence and co-operation of six Members of Parliament out of the ten Primitive Methodists who then had seats in the " House," emphasised the advanced development of Christian democracy amongst us.

The Great Cloud of Witnesses.—Dr. G. A. Gordon of Boston, U.S.A., in a recent volume* finely says : " The world of spirit is contemporaneous : God is the contemporary Deity ; the kingdom of souls is a reality in its own name and right, and we have to-day immediate access to this Reality, and may feel its pulses and powers in our heart of hearts." Was it such deep feelings as these which Dr. Rendel Harris had in his mind when he spoke of the forth-coming gathering of our people on Mow Hill as giving them an opportunity of being " baptised for the dead " ?   Such matters are almost too deep for words.   They can only just be glanced at in thought and left.   We have no apparatus for estimating the extent to which the Centenary Cele-

---

* *Aspects of the Infinite Mystery,* 1916, p. 191.

bration contributed to link us more closely with
that, by this time almost co-equal, part of our
Church who " have crossed the flood " and passed
out of sight, but not out of mind.

Unfulfilled Expectations. — As tabulated, the
spiritual results of the Centenary were disappointingly small. It had been hoped and expected that
there would be a large ingathering into the Church.
With this end in view the Evangelistic Committee
made the needful arrangements. Services that
sought to recall the fervour of the old days were
held throughout the country. " The Centenary
Revival " was given as the watchword. " Was it
too much," it was asked, " to hope and expect that
these years should bring up the membership to
250,000 ? "   But it was not to be. Spiritually they
were " lean years," not for our own Church only,
but for all the Churches ; and small consolation
was to be got out of the fact that we were in no worse
case than our neighbours. The Centenary years
passed, and the returns showed only eighteen more
members than in 1907, while the reports of the
General Sunday School Union frankly and feelingly
chronicled a decline. We say " feelingly," because
the pain it cost the writers to draw up these faith-
ful reports cannot be hidden. They seem to have
been written with a fluid more vital than ink. It
was puzzling and disappointing—this scanty
spiritual harvest of the Centenary years. It was
even humiliating. These feelings find poignant
expression in the Address to the Churches of 1909

prepared by M. P. Davison : " And yet, back of all this exuberance of feeling, there was a deep sense of humiliation and shame, that in the very midst of our Centenary celebrations we were confronted by figures that told of spiritual decline in nearly every department of our home-work. . . . We had hoped that in these exultant years we should not only have experienced a great uplift of spiritual life, but should have witnessed a large ingathering of souls into our Shiloh." There were deep searchings of heart ; probings into the causes of such a state of things. There may be a measure of truth in some or all of the explanations put forward. But we think time is showing more and more clearly that the condition of the Churches in the Centenary years was only part of the much larger question—the condition of England herself in those years. But more on this in the Epilogue which follows.

Epilogue.

I. ON-THE-EVE-OF-THE-WAR YEARS : 1913—JUNE 1914.

The End of a Curious Period.—For our nation
these two years were to prove the end of a period
closing in an abrupt and convulsive fashion that
took the bulk of people by surprise. That period
is separated from us as by a ": Great Divide " and
looks strangely remote now—so remote that, as one
has put it, those ante-bellum days might belong to
the days of George IV, rather than of George V
By contrast with the years that followed, the period
in question has strongly drawn the attention of
men. It has piqued their curiosity to a remarkable degree. Nobody seems to have a good word
for the period. This might easily be shown by
a selection of passages from books, pamphlets and
articles written by men of the most diverse opinions
and belonging to the most opposite schools of thought.
Nominally, it was a time of peace. But if peace be
a state of mind, rather than the mere absence of
war, then England was not at peace within herself.

The doors of the temple of Janus might be shut—
but Peace ?—no. There was Dublin gun-running
and the annoyance of the recurring suffragette raids.
They were " hectic times." " There was an ignoble
and fatuous pursuit of pleasure and profit." In
such terms as these have those days been described.
No lack of " envy, hatred and uncharitableness "
either, in those days. The feeling between
capitalists and wage-earners was embittered ; so
much so that, as we have just learned from
Mr. J. H. Thomas, it was only the coming of the
War that prevented a supreme effort being made
in the winter of 1914 to bring about a change in the
industrial situation ; and that would have meant
revolution. To borrow a phrase now familiar
in regard to the things of the spirit, it was a time
of " low visibility." The far spiritual horizons
contracted. The stars of the absolute heavens
were lost sight of, and only half aware of their loss
men declined on the seen and temporal. An era of
practical materialism, with its perturbing divisive
influences, seemed to have set in. Those who
were no friends of Great Britain whispered in
one another's ears the ominous word " decadence."
It almost looked as though the verdict were true
so long as you went by what you read in the daily
newspaper, as it chronicled the doings and mis-
doings, the bickerings and heated discussions, the
shekel-gathering, the pleasure-hunting that were
characteristic of the time. Thank God ! the
mischief had not gone too deep for recovery.
Beneath the surface, though sadly overlaid, there

M

were still moral forces that could be roused and assert their power. But as yet, we say, it was a time of "low visibility." History shows that we cannot escape such fluctuations. There are ebbs and flows, fat years and lean years. The Jubilee of our Church happily fell on a time of "high visibility" —of quickened response to spiritual influences. Then, the years 1858 to 1861 saw 21,428 added to our Church roll; but the financial results were meagre. It was precisely the reverse, as we have seen, during the Centenary years. Then the spiritual gains were almost negligible, while the financial results were impressively large. Both in explaining and passing strictures on the condition of the Churches in the ante-bellum period, the peculiar time-spirit of the period must be allowed for. In favouring times, as Archbishop Leighton says: "The Church may dilate more, and build as it were into breadth; but in trouble it rises more in height."

The Conferences of 1913–14 *on Peace and War.*— The years 1913 and 1914 have every appearance of beginning, in a natural way, a new period. As our fathers might have put it: The good ship "Primitive," refitted and revictualled, now taut and trim, began what was destined to be a momentous voyage. Officers and men were buoyant and hopeful, little knowing what new latitudes they would enter upon, and what strange entries would have to be made in the log. The "lean years" were not yet overpassed; yet, despite this disquieting fact, a spirit of hopefulness is recognisable. You note the sense of recovery, the feeling that the worst is past, the resolve to push the aggressive work, and to take advantage of the promising openings which presented themselves in the South Yorkshire Coal Field, at Cambridge, at Letchworth Garden City, St. Anne's and elsewhere. The enthusiasm in the cause of foreign missions was still rising and reacting favourably on the Home-work. But it is with the Pacifism that was so markedly in evidence at these two Conferences we are now concerned. It is one of the little ironies of our history that the Conference Minutes of 1913 should contain a long resolution on Peace, and those of 1914 a shorter one on Armaments, the latter of which is thus referred to in the Address to the Churches :—

" The Conference pronounced a judgment also on the alarming increase of armaments. The spirit underlying this is utterly sordid, and the war-scares are manufactured by great syndicates whose only object is to add to their already swollen dividends. These huge commercial trusts are amongst the direct foes of the Christian Gospel, and of the social progress of the nation."

It is obvious our chief Assembly had no suspicion of the storm that was brewing just across the North Sea that would burst " with hideous ruin and combustion " in less than two months of the closing of its sessions. It is not so obvious how the Primitive Methodists had come to be probably the most pronouncedly Pacifist denomination in the land save the Society of Friends. True ; it has been pointed out by an eminent authority that

" the wave of Pacifism which had been gathering strength for twenty-five years reached its height " about this time. But then it was strongly pacifist in sentiment long before this " wave " had begun its course, as has been already remarked (p. 115). But history shows, and the memory of some who read these lines will confirm it, there was an earlier wave of Pacifism about the time of the Great Exhibition of 1851—a wave to which the vigorous oratory of Cobden and Bright gave momentum; nor are there wanting signs that Primitive Methodism caught the swirl of that wave. Be this as it may, there is no room for doubt where our Church stood in regard to Peace or War in June 1914; yet, while the ink of the President's signature in the Conference Journal was still fresh, the bloodiest and most gigantic war in history broke out, and Primitive Methodists in their thousands were joining up. There was no mistake : we were " in the war," and the rest of the Free Churches were in it with us. It is not a charge of inconsistency on the part of our denominational leaders we are constructing. Far otherwise. Their known intense love of peace to the very outbreak of the War raises a strong presumption that only reasons of the most compelling kind will explain their action at this grave conjuncture. They rightly felt that the situation was without precedent ; that theories which left no room for this grim and grisly fact must be inadequate. It was idle saying " they had no use for the War." They could not dismiss it as an immense irrelevance. They had pondered deeply ; and really they could find no flaw in their country's case for war. It did seem that for once —and that was now—England could rightly call upon all her sons to help her lift up the standard against the enemy that was coming in as a flood. At last England was undertaking a war that, without any touch of irony, might be called a Crusade, a war untainted by selfish aims, a war based on sheer justice, and involving the future freedom and peace of the world and the interests of the kingdom of God. The flock over which they had watched had divined rightly, and obeyed a sure instinct in. rallying to the colours, and they must stand by their flock and accept the stern call of duty, however painful it might be. They loved and longed for Peace as much as ever, and now God was asking " How much are you prepared to do and dare and suffer in order to bring the long reign of Peace on the earth ? " These were probably some of the thoughts revolving in the minds of our leaders in the opening weeks of the great world-tragedy. In the conclusion reached we see consistency at its highest and best.

II. PRIMITIVE METHODISM IN TIME OF WAR.

" Once to every man and nation comes the moment to decide,
In the strife of truth with falsehood, for the good or evil side.
Some great cause, God's new Messiah, offering each the bloom
　　or blight,
And the choice goes by for ever 'twixt that darkness and that
　　light."
　　　　　　　　　　　　　　　　　　　LOWELL.

We have now completed the task we set ourselves —to outline the course of Primitive Methodism from its first perceptible beginnings in 1800 to 1914 ; to give some idea of its extension or " dilation " (to use again Leighton's word), and, what is more, its enlargement in the sphere of ideas and in the range of its activities. From the well-head of Primitive Methodism on Mow Cop to Holborn Hall and to the verge of " the Great Divide " of the War is a long journey, often an arduous one and not without its perils and sufferings, but, quite as certainly, a journey taken under evident tokens of divine leadership. Of the War, what can be said except in the most general way ? To do more is impossible, and to indulge in speculations and forecasts concerning the changes the War not yet ended will bring about would be futile. All that can be attempted here is briefly to indicate how Primitive Methodism stood in relation to the War, and how its attitude found official expression in 1915 and 1918 ; to glance at what has been our part in the War in the way of service and suffering ; and what the War has done for us. It will be for our encouragement if, in these sorely distressful times, we can in any measure appropriate the poet's line—" Find in loss a gain to match."

The First War Conference of 1915 was held at Reading. It is a coincidence that its President, J. Day Thompson, sat as a delegate at the important Conference of 1885—the one which saw the feeble beginnings of Army-work. What a change thirty years had brought about ! When the Conference assembled we were as a Church committed to the

War. Heavy pledges had been given. When the Missionary Report was drawn up for Conference it was stated that twenty thousand Primitive Methodists had joined the colours. But when the Reading Conference met that number had been far exceeded ; and still the stream of volunteers was flowing—from many a manse and Sunday School and Christian Endeavour and Choir. Eight Huts had been set up in various military centres through the liberality of our people since October 1914, when the scheme for making such needful provision was launched with enthusiasm. Something bigger even than this—the formation of a United Board—had been done. How this was brought about the following extract from the General Missionary Secretary's Report to the Conference will show :—

" The greatest event in our Home Missionary Department has undoubtedly been the creation of an Army Department. Great crises test institutions as well as individuals. When the War broke out we had no authorised Chaplains, either to the Army or the Navy. For years we have done work among the soldiers at Aldershot without Government recognition. New conditions were created by the War. From every Station news came of our young men joining the Colours, and the need for us to provide for their social and spiritual welfare was immediate and imperative. The first step was to seek Government recognition and claim equal treatment with other religious bodies. This was rendered the easier by the adoption of a suggestion made by the Rev. J. H. Shakespeare that the Baptists, Congregationalists, United Methodists and Primitive Methodists should unite under a representative Army Board to minister to the spiritual needs of the soldiers of these several Churches. This was happily done, and has resulted in a friendly alliance which may have wide-reaching consequences in days to come."

The Report adds that already seven chaplains and

upwards of seventy-seven officiating clergymen had been appointed. When the Conference closed, the number of chaplains had been increased to twelve.

Besides endorsing and recording what the General Missionary Committee had done in urgent and unprecedented circumstances, the Conference, as in duty bound, in a carefully considered Resolution, left no room for doubt where the Primitive Methodist Church stood in relation to the War. This Resolution, together with the Ex-President's Address to the Churches, are historic documents, and doubtless will be regarded and treated as such in the years to come by our denominational historians. For our purpose it will suffice if we give the opening and concluding paragraphs of the Resolution :

" That this Annual Conference of the Primitive Methodist Church views with grief and horror the European War, and regards as guilty of treason to Christian civilisation, those who have provoked this awful conflict.

" We believe in the sanctity of peace, and would strive to enthrone the will of the Son of Man among the nations. We acknowledge the efforts made for peace by our King, his Government, and especially by the Secretary of State for Foreign Affairs.

" This hideous calamity has been forced upon us by the brutal arrogance and lawless ambition of a military caste, and a materialistic philosophy which would, if triumphant, fling the world back into the most piteous savagery. We have been called to resistance by sacred claims of honour, by the impulse of fidelity to international relations, and by the urgent need of small nations. We support His Majesty's Government in its call to Britain to spare neither blood nor treasure to crush the German conspiracy against the freedom and peace of the world."

.   .   .   .

" We declare our faith in God and in the certain triumph of His Kingdom. Through the strife of principalities and powers, and the grave endurance of a suffering that is sacramental, civilisation shall be cleansed, the reign of righteousness shall be secured, and the Divine Will done on earth as it is in heaven."

When, in June 1918, the Conference met at Northampton it had the retrospect of close upon four years of war, and of Church-life under war conditions. The denomination had taken its course and held to it. In the extract we have to give from the "Pastoral" written by Ex-President J. Tolefree Parr, we fail to detect any signs of faltering conviction in the righteousness of the War or any slackening of effort in doing what we could to help bring the War to a victorious and righteous conclusion. Indeed, the longer the War had lasted and the more it had widened, the more, inversely, it seemed to have narrowed down to be a supreme struggle for ascendency between moral and material forces. The extract which follows is also valuable as a record for another reason : By the facts and figures it gives we gain a vivid idea of the toll in precious human lives and suffering our Church was paying for her participation in the War.

" The Conference placed on record its admiration for the heroic sons of our Church who are engaged in deadly combat with a ruthless enemy, and expressed its deep sympathy with all our beloved people who have been called upon to share in the poignant sorrows and crucial sacrifices of the nation.

"No less than 150,000 Primitive Methodists have joined the Army and Navy, including upwards of 4,000 local preachers. Forty-three ministers have served as chaplains, and nearly 200 as officiating clergymen. In the various philanthropic and beneficent ministries of the war our people have nobly borne their part. A solemn and impressive Conference Service was held in memory of 15,000 brave sons of our Church, ' who in this great hour of Destiny have given themselves for England and humanity, and who, having made the supreme sacrifice, are now assembled as God's happy warriors on the Plains of Peace ' clothed in the white robes of immortality.   The truths taught them in the Sabbath School enabled them to meet death with calm assurance.   They shared the faith of Rupert Brooke, the poet, who, just before he fell mortally wounded at Lemnos, wrote on a scrap of paper :

> ' Safe where no safety is, safe though I fall;
> And if these poor limbs die, safest of all.' "

The tone and proceedings of the Northampton Conference of 1918 should serve to check any tendency to take gloomy views of the future of Primitive Methodism.   It was indeed one of the most remarkable Conferences in our history, and it is good to let the mind linger on it as we approach the end of our task.   When we recollect that the Conference came together in the midst of the anxieties and dislocations caused by a long War, the description of it as " The Wonderful Conference " seems amply justified.   One cannot but feel there must have been some hidden spiritual conduit to which the Northampton friends, with their " Lightning Fund," and the Conference, with its missionary enthusiasm, its generosity and its far-sighted legislative enactments, had direct access.   It did seem as though the War which had brought so much evil and suffering had been compelled to bring along with them rich compensations.

Compensations.—The Great Revival that was the burthen of our prayers in the Centenary years came, but not in the way we thought it would. We had figured to ourselves a Revival of the old type—visiting our denominational enclosure as in

former days. Whereas it came as a John-the-
Baptist Revival to rouse half the world and to do
rough preparatory root-work. The War came as a
shock to England and roused her from her decadent
mood. The shock liberated the great, though
simple, imperatives which lie at the roots of man's
nature. These were not dead, as in our little faith
we had been tempted to believe. The Church's
witness and teaching had gone further than she
knew, and had helped to keep these moral imperatives alive. The shock of War quickened them.
There was a great moral revulsion, followed by a
great moral resolution. " I will arise and resist
this Colossus of Materialism threatening to bestride
half the world and subdue it to his merciless will."
When, in scorn of consequences, wrong, cruelty,
injustice are resisted, there must needs be suffering.
But they who resist and suffer are in the right
direction. They are in line with Christ and His
Cross and cannot fail of the consolation which
attends suffering for righteousness' sake. If this
indeed be true, it ought not to appear strange that
in such a war as this there should be compensations,
old truths revitalised, wider horizons opening to
view, a firmer grip of immortality ; or that in the
homes of bereavement and distress the consolations
of the accepted Cross should "much more abound."

Some Other Gains of the War.—We have had to
chronicle the successive enlargements of sphere
and idea to which Primitive Methodism has attained
during her more than a century of history. The

latest of these remains to be noted and emphasised. The War has helped to make our Church more National than, a few years ago, she could even have dreamed of becoming. For four years we have been in the full tide of the nation's life, and never again, it is to be hoped, shall we subside into its shallows. Even if we should be called upon to oppose, we shall still be a recognised part of "His Majesty's Opposition." With his usual acumen, Ex-President G. Bennett fastened upon this war-brought change in his Address to the Churches of the first War Conference. A finer Address and one more appropriate to the circumstances under which it was written could not have been penned. One sentence we cannot forbear quoting; "The righteousness of the War has made the Church more National than ever she has been, and has made her conscious not only of herself, but that she has her part to take in the greater life of her country."

Like a heavy "barrage" the War has already levelled many things. Surely we may hope it may level some at least of the most flagrant denominational barriers and thus take out of the way what is increasingly felt to be a hindrance and a reproach. We may hope, too, it will lead us to simplify our creed. One of the preoccupations of these years has been the revision of the Deed Poll and the preparation of our Credal Standard. It is held up by the War. That is well. It will be better still if we take thought, lay it aside, and, learning by experience, put the living Christ in the place of our creed and get the other Churches to do the same.

What higher demand can we make of any man than that he shall be willing to avow before his fellows that he knows " Whom he has believed," and that he takes Christ as Saviour and Lord, his pattern and his power ?

The Call of the Future.—This final paragraph is penned when the great War is over. November 11th, 1918, will be a memorable day in history. The War has ended as no one ever dared to dream. The Central Powers have collapsed, and accepted terms of armistice which are tantamount to unconditional surrender. Most wonderful of all, the path is now open for the settlement of European politics, and indeed of politics internationally, on the lines of righteousness, truth and peace. The League of Nations is the aim of the Allies, and of the United States of America, and what this will mean the most optimistic can scarcely suggest. It means that wars will cease, that the very spirit of militarism will be exorcised, that all nations will turn more and more to domestic arts, and commercial and educational pursuits. With this incubus removed, the world will pass into a safer and saner place.

Now is the time for the churches also to advance. The churches need to clarify their ideals in the light of the life and teaching of the Master. The church should be the conscience of the nation. There are signs that the churches have been preparing for this great hour. Readjustments will be necessary, but most of all a new baptism is required. For spiritual triumphs, we must work on spiritual lines and in spiritual forces. As part of the universal Church of Christ we have our part to play in the new time that is dawning. In the days of our fathers, they were marvellously wide-awake, quick to discern the signs of the times, and full of adaptiveness and ingenuity. That is the temper the new day demands. Our own church will be quickened by the home-coming of those who have served on the land, on the sea, and in the air. With their widened experience, and their deepened sense of the gravity of life, they will bring fresh currents of thought, and potent influences of service into the churches to which before the war and through the war, they have belonged. A finer quality of manhood and womanhood is a clamant call of this unique time. The ideal of the church is to inspire its members with the ethics of Jesus, and send them out into the world, to live on His lines, and to see that His programme is fulfilled. In the assurance that He is with us always we may " greet the unseen with a cheer."

The writer, in laying aside his pen—probably for good and all—confesses himself an unrepentant optimist in regard to his Church. He believes that Primitive Methodism will give proof that she has not lost her old-time flexibility—her power to adapt herself to changed conditions.

FINIS.

For EU product safety concerns, contact us at Calle de José Abascal, 56–1°,
28003 Madrid, Spain or eugpsr@cambridge.org.

www.ingramcontent.com/pod-product-compliance
Ingram Content Group UK Ltd.
Pitfield, Milton Keynes, MK11 3LW, UK
UKHW012343130625
459647UK00009B/487